Ingenious Strides for AI Driverless Cars

Practical Advances in Artificial Intelligence and Machine Learning

Dr. Lance B. Eliot, MBA, PhD

ISBN: 1-7329760-2-3
ISBN-13: 978-1-7329760-2-3

DEDICATION

To my incredible daughter, Lauren, and my incredible son, Michael.

Forest fortuna adiuvat (from the Latin; good fortune favors the brave).

CONTENTS

Chapters

Lance B. Eliot

ACKNOWLEDGMENTS

I have been the beneficiary of advice and counsel by many friends, colleagues, family, investors, and many others. I want to thank everyone that has aided me throughout my career. I write from the heart and the head, having experienced first-hand what it means to have others around you that support you during the good times and the tough times.

To Warren Bennis, one of my doctoral advisors and ultimately a colleague, I offer my deepest thanks and appreciation, especially for his calm and insightful wisdom and support.

To Mark Stevens and his generous efforts toward funding and supporting the USC Stevens Center for Innovation.

To Lloyd Greif and the USC Lloyd Greif Center for Entrepreneurial Studies for their ongoing encouragement of founders and entrepreneurs.

To Peter Drucker, William Wang, Aaron Levie, Peter Kim, Jon Kraft, Cindy Crawford, Jenny Ming, Steve Milligan, Chis Underwood, Frank Gehry, Buzz Aldrin, Steve Forbes, Bill Thompson, Dave Dillon, Alan Fuerstman, Larry Ellison, Jim Sinegal, John Sperling, Mark Stevenson, Anand Nallathambi, Thomas Barrack, Jr., and many other innovators and leaders that I have met and gained mightily from doing so.

Thanks to Ed Trainor, Kevin Anderson, James Hickey, Wendell Jones, Ken Harris, DuWayne Peterson, Mike Brown, Jim Thornton, Abhi Beniwal, Al Biland, John Nomura, Eliot Weinman, John Desmond, and many others for their unwavering support during my career.

And most of all thanks as always to Michael and Lauren, for their ongoing support and for having seen me writing and heard much of this material during the many months involved in writing it. To their patience and willingness to listen.

Lance B. Eliot

INTRODUCTION

This is a book that provides the newest innovations and the latest Artificial Intelligence (AI) advances about the emerging nature of AI-based autonomous self-driving driverless cars. Via recent advances in Artificial Intelligence (AI) and Machine Learning (ML), we are nearing the day when vehicles can control themselves and will not require and nor rely upon human intervention to perform their driving tasks (or, that <u>allow</u> for human intervention, but only *require* human intervention in very limited ways).

Similar to my other related books, which I describe in a moment and list the chapters in the Appendix A of this book, I am particularly focused on those advances that pertain to self-driving cars. The phrase "autonomous vehicles" is often used to refer to any kind of vehicle, whether it is ground-based or in the air or sea, and whether it is a cargo hauling trailer truck or a conventional passenger car. Though the aspects described in this book are certainly applicable to all kinds of autonomous vehicles, I am focused more so here on cars.

Indeed, I am especially known for my role in aiding the advancement of self-driving cars, serving currently as the Executive Director of the Cybernetic Self-Driving Cars Institute.. In addition to writing software, designing and developing systems and software for self-driving cars, I also speak and write quite a bit about the topic. This book is a collection of some of my more advanced essays. For those of you that might have seen my essays posted elsewhere, I have updated them and integrated them into this book as one handy cohesive package.

You might be interested in companion books that I have written that provide additional key innovations and fundamentals about self-driving cars. Those books are entitled **"Introduction to Driverless Self-Driving Cars," "Advances in AI and Autonomous Vehicles: Cybernetic Self-Driving Cars," "Self-Driving Cars: "The Mother of All AI Projects," "Innovation and Thought Leadership on Self-Driving Driverless Cars," "New Advances in AI Autonomous Driverless Self-Driving Cars,"** and **"Autonomous Vehicle Driverless Self-Driving Cars and**

Artificial Intelligence," "Transformative Artificial Intelligence Driverless Self-Driving Cars," "Disruptive Artificial Intelligence and Driverless Self-Driving Cars, and "State-of-the-Art AI Driverless Self-Driving Cars," and "Top Trends in AI Self-Driving Cars," and "AI Innovations and Self-Driving Cars," "Crucial Advances for AI Driverless Cars," "Sociotechnical Insights and AI Driverless Cars," "Pioneering Advances for AI Driverless Cars" and "Leading Edge Trends for AI Driverless Cars," "The Cutting Edge of AI Autonomous Cars" and "The Next Wave of AI Self-Driving Cars" and "Revolutionary Innovations of AI Self-Driving Cars," and "AI Self-Driving Cars Breakthroughs," "Trailblazing Trends for AI Self-Driving Cars" and "Ingenious Strides for AI Driverless Cars" (they are all available via Amazon). See Appendix A of this herein book to see a listing of the chapters covered in those three books.

For the introduction here to this book, I am going to borrow my introduction from those companion books, since it does a good job of laying out the landscape of self-driving cars and my overall viewpoints on the topic. The remainder of the book is all new material that does not appear in the companion books.

INTRODUCTION TO SELF-DRIVING CARS

This is a book about self-driving cars. Someday in the future, we'll all have self-driving cars and this book will perhaps seem antiquated, but right now, we are at the forefront of the self-driving car wave. Daily news bombards us with flashes of new announcements by one car maker or another and leaves the impression that within the next few weeks or maybe months that the self-driving car will be here. A casual non-technical reader would assume from these news flashes that in fact we must be on the cusp of a true self-driving car.

Here's a real news flash: We are still quite a distance from having a true self-driving car. It is years to go before we get there.

Why is that? Because a true self-driving car is akin to a moonshot. In the same manner that getting us to the moon was an incredible feat, likewise can it be said for achieving a true self-driving car. Anybody that suggests or even brashly states that the true self-driving car is nearly here should be viewed with great skepticism. Indeed, you'll see that I often tend to use the word "hogwash" or "crock" when I assess much of the decidedly *fake news* about self-driving cars. Those of us on the inside know that what is often reported to the outside is malarkey. Few of the insiders are willing to say so. I have no such hesitation.

Indeed, I've been writing a popular blog post about self-driving cars and hitting hard on those that try to wave their hands and pretend that we are on the imminent verge of true self-driving cars. For many years, I've been known as the AI Insider. Besides writing about AI, I also develop AI software. I do what I describe. It also gives me insights into what others that are doing AI are really doing versus what it is said they are doing.

Many faithful readers had asked me to pull together my insightful short essays and put them into another book, which you are now holding.

For those of you that have been reading my essays over the years, this collection not only puts them together into one handy package, I also updated the essays and added new material. For those of you that are new to the topic of self-driving cars and AI, I hope you find these essays approachable and informative. I also tend to have a writing style with a bit of a voice, and so you'll see that I am times have a wry sense of humor and poke at conformity.

As a former professor and founder of an AI research lab, I for many years wrote in the formal language of academic writing. I published in referred journals and served as an editor for several AI journals. This writing here is not of the nature, and I have adopted a different and more informal style for these essays. That being said, I also do mention from time-to-time more rigorous material on AI and encourage you all to dig into those deeper and more formal materials if so interested.

I am also an AI practitioner. This means that I write AI software for a living. Currently, I head-up the Cybernetics Self-Driving Car Institute, where we are developing AI software for self-driving cars. I am excited to also report that my son, also a software engineer, heads-up our Cybernetics Self-Driving Car Lab. What I have helped to start, and for which he is an integral part, ultimately he will carry long into the future after I have retired. My daughter, a marketing whiz, also is integral to our efforts as head of our Marketing group. She too will carry forward the legacy now being formulated.

For those of you that are reading this book and have a penchant for writing code, you might consider taking a look at the open source code available for self-driving cars. This is a handy place to start learning how to develop AI for self-driving cars. There are also many new educational courses spring forth. There is a growing body of those wanting to learn about and develop self-driving cars, and a growing body of colleges, labs, and other avenues by which you can learn about self-driving cars.

This book will provide a foundation of aspects that I think will get you ready for those kinds of more advanced training opportunities. If you've already taken those classes, you'll likely find these essays especially interesting as they offer a perspective that I am betting few other instructors or faculty offered to you. These are challenging essays that ask you to think beyond the conventional about self-driving cars.

THE MOTHER OF ALL AI PROJECTS

In June 2017, Apple CEO Tim Cook came out and finally admitted that Apple has been working on a self-driving car. As you'll see in my essays, Apple was enmeshed in secrecy about their self-driving car efforts. We have only been able to read the tea leaves and guess at what Apple has been up to. The notion of an iCar has been floating for quite a while, and self-driving engineers and researchers have been signing tight-lipped Non-Disclosure Agreements (NDA's) to work on projects at Apple that were as shrouded in mystery as any military invasion plans might be.

Tim Cook said something that many others in the Artificial Intelligence (AI) field have been saying, namely, the creation of a self-driving car has got to be the mother of all AI projects. In other words, it is in fact a tremendous moonshot for AI. If a self-driving car can be crafted and the AI works as we hope, it means that we have made incredible strides with AI and that therefore it opens many other worlds of potential breakthrough accomplishments that AI can solve.

Is this hyperbole? Am I just trying to make AI seem like a miracle worker and so provide self-aggrandizing statements for those of us writing the AI software for self-driving cars? No, it is not hyperbole. Developing a true self-driving car is really, really, really hard to do. Let me take a moment to explain why. As a side note, I realize that the Apple CEO is known for at times uttering hyperbole, and he had previously said for example that the year 2012 was "the mother of all years," and he had said that the release of iOS 10 was "the mother of all releases" – all of which does suggest he likes to use the handy "mother of" expression. But, I assure you, in terms of true self-driving cars, he has hit the nail on the head. For sure.

When you think about a moonshot and how we got to the moon, there are some identifiable characteristics and those same aspects can be applied to creating a true self-driving car. You'll notice that I keep putting the word "true" in front of the self-driving car expression. I do so because as per my essay about the various levels of self-driving cars, there are some self-driving cars that are only somewhat of a self-driving car. The somewhat versions are ones that require a human driver to be ready to intervene. In my view, that's not a true self-driving car. A true self-driving car is one that requires no human driver intervention at all. It is a car that can entirely undertake via automation the driving task without any human driver needed. This is the essence of what is known as a Level 5 self-driving car. We are currently at the Level 2 and Level 3 mark, and not yet at Level 5.

Getting to the moon involved aspects such as having big stretch goals, incremental progress, experimentation, innovation, and so on. Let's review how this applied to the moonshot of the bygone era, and how it applies to the self-driving car moonshot of today.

Big Stretch Goal

Trying to take a human and deliver the human to the moon, and bring them back, safely, was an extremely large stretch goal at the time. No one knew whether it could be done. The technology wasn't available yet. The cost was huge. The determination would need to be fierce. Etc. To reach a Level 5 self-driving car is going to be the same. It is a big stretch goal. We can readily get to the Level 3, and we are able to see the Level 4 just up ahead, but a Level 5 is still an unknown as to if it is doable. It should eventually be doable and in the same way that we thought we'd eventually get to the moon, but when it will occur is a different story.

Incremental Progress

Getting to the moon did not happen overnight in one fell swoop. It took years and years of incremental progress to get there. Likewise for self-driving cars. Google has famously been striving to get to the Level 5, and pretty much been willing to forgo dealing with the intervening levels, but most of the other self-driving car makers are doing the incremental route. Let's get a good Level 2 and a somewhat Level 3 going. Then, let's improve the Level 3 and get a somewhat Level 4 going. Then, let's improve the Level 4 and finally arrive at a Level 5. This seems to be the prevalent way that we are going to achieve the true self-driving car.

Experimentation

You likely know that there were various experiments involved in perfecting the approach and technology to get to the moon. As per making incremental progress, we first tried to see if we could get a rocket to go into space and safety return, then put a monkey in there, then with a human, then we went all the way to the moon but didn't land, and finally we arrived at the mission that actually landed on the moon. Self-driving cars are the same way. We are doing simulations of self-driving cars. We do testing of self-driving cars on private land under controlled situations. We do testing of self-driving cars on public roadways, often having to meet regulatory requirements including for example having an engineer or equivalent in the car to take over the controls if needed. And so on. Experiments big and small are needed to figure out what works and what doesn't.

Innovation

There are already some advances in AI that are allowing us to progress toward self-driving cars. We are going to need even more advances. Innovation in all aspects of technology are going to be required to achieve a true self-driving car. By no means do we already have everything in-hand that we need to get there. Expect new inventions and new approaches, new algorithms, etc.

Setbacks

Most of the pundits are avoiding talking about potential setbacks in the progress toward self-driving cars. Getting to the moon involved many setbacks, some of which you never have heard of and were buried at the time so as to not dampen enthusiasm and funding for getting to the moon. A recurring theme in many of my included essays is that there are going to be setbacks as we try to arrive at a true self-driving car. Take a deep breath and be ready. I just hope the setbacks don't completely stop progress. I am sure that it will cause progress to alter in a manner that we've not yet seen in the self-driving car field. I liken the self-driving car of today to the excitement everyone had for Uber when it first got going. Today, we have a different view of Uber and with each passing day there are more regulations to the ride sharing business and more concerns raised. The darling child only stays a darling until finally that child acts up. It will happen the same with self-driving cars.

SELF-DRIVING CARS CHALLENGES

But what exactly makes things so hard to have a true self-driving car, you might be asking. You have seen cruise control for years and years. You've lately seen cars that can do parallel parking. You've seen YouTube videos of Tesla drivers that put their hands out the window as their car zooms along the highway, and seen to therefore be in a self-driving car. Aren't we just needing to put a few more sensors onto a car and then we'll have in-hand a true self-driving car? Nope.

Consider for a moment the nature of the driving task. We don't just let anyone at any age drive a car. Worldwide, most countries won't license a driver until the age of 18, though many do allow a learner's permit at the age of 15 or 16. Some suggest that a younger age would be physically too small to reach the controls of the car. Though this might be the case, we could easily adjust the controls to allow for younger aged and thus smaller stature. It's not their physical size that matters. It's their cognitive development that matters.

To drive a car, you need to be able to reason about the car, what the car can and cannot do. You need to know how to operate the car. You need to know about how other cars on the road drive. You need to know what is allowed in driving such as speed limits and driving within marked lanes. You need to be able to react to situations and be able to avoid getting into accidents. You need to ascertain when to hit your brakes, when to steer clear of a pedestrian, and how to keep from ramming that motorcyclist that just cut you off.

Many of us had taken courses on driving. We studied about driving and took driver training. We had to take a test and pass it to be able to drive. The point being that though most adults take the driving task for granted, and we often "mindlessly" drive our cars, there is a significant amount of cognitive effort that goes into driving a car. After a while, it becomes second nature. You don't especially think about how you drive, you just do it. But, if you watch a novice driver, say a teenager learning to drive, you suddenly realize that there is a lot more complexity to it than we seem to realize.

Furthermore, driving is a very serious task. I recall when my daughter and son first learned to drive. They are both very conscientious people. They wanted to make sure that whatever they did, they did well, and that they did not harm anyone. Every day, when you get into a car, it is probably around 4,000 pounds of hefty metal and plastics (about two tons), and it is a lethal weapon. Think about it. You drive down the street in an object that weighs two tons and with the engine it can accelerate and ram into anything you want to hit. The damage a car can inflict is very scary. Both my children were surprised that they were being given the right to maneuver this monster of a beast that could cause tremendous harm entirely by merely letting go of the steering wheel for a moment or taking your eyes off the road.

In fact, in the United States alone there are about 30,000 deaths per year by auto accidents, which is around 100 per day. Given that there are about 263 million cars in the United States, I am actually more amazed that the number of fatalities is not a lot higher. During my morning commute, I look at all the thousands of cars on the freeway around me, and I think that if all of them decided to go zombie and drive in a crazy maniac way, there would be many people dead. Somehow, incredibly, each day, most people drive relatively safely. To me, that's a miracle right there. Getting millions and millions of people to be safe and sane when behind the wheel of a two ton mobile object, it's a feat that we as a society should admire with pride.

So, hopefully you are in agreement that the driving task requires a great deal of cognition. You don't' need to be especially smart to drive a car, and we've done quite a bit to make car driving viable for even the average dolt. There isn't an IQ test that you need to take to drive a car. If you can read and write, and pass a test, you pretty much can legally drive a car. There are of course some that drive a car and are not legally permitted to do so, plus there are private areas such as farms where drivers are young, but for public roadways in the United States, you can be generally of average intelligence (or less) and be able to legally drive.

This though makes it seem like the cognitive effort must not be much. If the cognitive effort was truly hard, wouldn't we only have Einstein's that could drive a car? We have made sure to keep the driving task as simple as we can, by making the controls easy and relatively standardized, and by having roads that are relatively standardized, and so on. It is as though Disneyland has put their Autopia into the real-world, by us all as a society agreeing that roads will be a certain way, and we'll all abide by the various rules of driving.

A modest cognitive task by a human is still something that stymies AI. You certainly know that AI has been able to beat chess players and be good at other kinds of games. This type of narrow cognition is not what car driving is about. Car driving is much wider. It requires knowledge about the world, which a chess playing AI system does not need to know. The cognitive aspects of driving are on the one hand seemingly simple, but at the same time require layer upon layer of knowledge about cars, people, roads, rules, and a myriad of other "common sense" aspects. We don't have any AI systems today that have that same kind of breadth and depth of awareness and knowledge.

As revealed in my essays, the self-driving car of today is using trickery to do particular tasks. It is all very narrow in operation. Plus, it currently assumes that a human driver is ready to intervene. It is like a child that we have taught to stack blocks, but we are needed to be right there in case the child stacks them too high and they begin to fall over. AI of today is brittle, it is narrow, and it does not approach the cognitive abilities of humans. This is why the true self-driving car is somewhere out in the future.

Another aspect to the driving task is that it is not solely a mind exercise. You do need to use your senses to drive. You use your eyes a vision sensors to see the road ahead. You vision capability is like a streaming video, which your brain needs to continually analyze as you drive. Where is the road? Is there a pedestrian in the way? Is there another car ahead of you? Your senses are relying a flood of info to your brain. Self-driving cars are trying to do the same, by using cameras, radar, ultrasound, and lasers. This is an attempt at mimicking how humans have senses and sensory apparatus.

Thus, the driving task is mental and physical. You use your senses, you use your arms and legs to manipulate the controls of the car, and you use your brain to assess the sensory info and direct your limbs to act upon the controls of the car. This all happens instantly. If you've ever perhaps gotten something in your eye and only had one eye available to drive with, you suddenly realize how dependent upon vision you are. If you have a broken foot with a cast, you suddenly realize how hard it is to control the brake pedal and the accelerator. If you've taken medication and your brain is maybe sluggish, you suddenly realize how much mental strain is required to drive a car.

An AI system that plays chess only needs to be focused on playing chess. The physical aspects aren't important because usually a human moves the chess pieces or the chessboard is shown on an electronic display. Using AI for a more life-and-death task such as analyzing MRI images of patients, this again does not require physical capabilities and instead is done by examining images of bits.

Driving a car is a true life-and-death task. It is a use of AI that can easily and at any moment produce death. For those colleagues of mine that are developing this AI, as am I, we need to keep in mind the somber aspects of this. We are producing software that will have in its virtual hands the lives of the occupants of the car, and the lives of those in other nearby cars, and the lives of nearby pedestrians, etc. Chess is not usually a life-or-death matter.

Driving is all around us. Cars are everywhere. Most of today's AI applications involve only a small number of people. Or, they are behind the scenes and we as humans have other recourse if the AI messes up. AI that is driving a car at 80 miles per hour on a highway had better not mess up. The consequences are grave. Multiply this by the number of cars, if we could put magically self-driving into every car in the USA, we'd have AI running in the 263 million cars. That's a lot of AI spread around. This is AI on a massive scale that we are not doing today and that offers both promise and potential peril.

There are some that want AI for self-driving cars because they envision a world without any car accidents. They envision a world in which there is no car congestion and all cars cooperate with each other. These are wonderful utopian visions.

They are also very misleading. The adoption of self-driving cars is going to be incremental and not overnight. We cannot economically just junk all existing cars. Nor are we going to be able to affordably retrofit existing cars. It is more likely that self-driving cars will be built into new cars and that over many years of gradual replacement of existing cars that we'll see the mix of self-driving cars become substantial in the real-world.

In these essays, I have tried to offer technological insights without being overly technical in my description, and also blended the business, societal, and economic aspects too. Technologists need to consider the non-technological impacts of what they do. Non-technologists should be aware of what is being developed.

We all need to work together to collectively be prepared for the enormous disruption and transformative aspects of true self-driving cars. We all need to be involved in this mother of all AI projects.

WHAT THIS BOOK PROVIDES

What does this book provide to you? It introduces many of the key elements about self-driving cars and does so with an AI based perspective. I weave together technical and non-technical aspects, readily going from being concerned about the cognitive capabilities of the driving task and how the technology is embodying this into self-driving cars, and in the next breath I discuss the societal and economic aspects.

They are all intertwined because that's the way reality is. You cannot separate out the technology per se, and instead must consider it within the milieu of what is being invented and innovated, and do so with a mindset towards the contemporary mores and culture that shape what we are doing and what we hope to do.

WHY THIS BOOK

I wrote this book to try and bring to the public view many aspects about self-driving cars that nobody seems to be discussing.

For business leaders that are either involved in making self-driving cars or that are going to leverage self-driving cars, I hope that this book will enlighten you as to the risks involved and ways in which you should be strategizing about how to deal with those risks.

For entrepreneurs, startups and other businesses that want to enter into the self-driving car market that is emerging, I hope this book sparks your interest in doing so, and provides some sense of what might be prudent to pursue.

For researchers that study self-driving cars, I hope this book spurs your interest in the risks and safety issues of self-driving cars, and also nudges you toward conducting research on those aspects.

For students in computer science or related disciplines, I hope this book will provide you with interesting and new ideas and material, for which you might conduct research or provide some career direction insights for you.

For AI companies and high-tech companies pursuing self-driving cars, this book will hopefully broaden your view beyond just the mere coding and development needed to make self-driving cars.

For all readers, I hope that you will find the material in this book to be stimulating. Some of it will be repetitive of things you already know. But I am pretty sure that you'll also find various eureka moments whereby you'll discover a new technique or approach that you had not earlier thought of. I am also betting that there will be material that forces you to rethink some of your current practices.

I am not saying you will suddenly have an epiphany and change what you are doing. I do think though that you will reconsider or perhaps revisit what you are doing.

For anyone choosing to use this book for teaching purposes, please take a look at my suggestions for doing so, as described in the Appendix. I have found the material handy in courses that I have taught, and likewise other faculty have told me that they have found the material handy, in some cases as extended readings and in other instances as a core part of their course (depending on the nature of the class).

In my writing for this book, I have tried carefully to blend both the practitioner and the academic styles of writing. It is not as dense as is typical academic journal writing, but at the same time offers depth by going into the nuances and trade-offs of various practices.

The word "deep" is in vogue today, meaning getting deeply into a subject or topic, and so is the word "unpack" which means to tease out the underlying aspects of a subject or topic. I have sought to offer material that addresses an issue or topic by going relatively deeply into it and make sure that it is well unpacked.

Finally, in any book about AI, it is difficult to use our everyday words without having some of them be misinterpreted. Specifically, it is easy to anthropomorphize AI. When I say that an AI system "knows" something, I do not want you to construe that the AI system has sentience and "knows" in the same way that humans do. They aren't that way, as yet. I have tried to use quotes around such words from time-to-time to emphasize that the words I am using should not be misinterpreted to ascribe true human intelligence to the AI systems that we know of today. If I used quotes around all such words, the book would be very difficult to read, and so I am doing so judiciously. Please keep that in mind as you read the material, thanks.

Lance B. Eliot

COMPANION BOOKS

If you find this material of interest, you might enjoy these too:

1. **"Introduction to Driverless Self-Driving Cars"** by Dr. Lance Eliot

2. **"Innovation and Thought Leadership on Self-Driving Driverless Cars"** by Dr. Lance Eliot

3. **"Advances in AI and Autonomous Vehicles: Cybernetic Self-Driving Cars"** by Dr. Lance Eliot

4. **"Self-Driving Cars: The Mother of All AI Projects"** by Dr. Lance Eliot

5. **"New Advances in AI Autonomous Driverless Self-Driving Cars"** by Dr. Lance Eliot

6. **"Autonomous Vehicle Driverless Self-Driving Cars and Artificial Intelligence"** by Dr. Lance Eliot and Michael B. Eliot

7. **"Transformative Artificial Intelligence Driverless Self-Driving Cars"** by Dr. Lance Eliot

8. **"Disruptive Artificial Intelligence and Driverless Self-Driving Cars"** by Dr. Lance Eliot

9. "State-of-the-Art AI Driverless Self-Driving Cars" by Dr. Lance Eliot

10. **"Top Trends in AI Self-Driving Cars"** by Dr. Lance Eliot

11. **"AI Innovations and Self-Driving Cars"** by Dr. Lance Eliot

12. **"Crucial Advances for AI Driverless Cars"** by Dr. Lance Eliot

13. **"Sociotechnical Insights and AI Driverless Cars"** by Dr. Lance Eliot.

14. **"Pioneering Advances for AI Driverless Cars"** by Dr. Lance Eliot

15. **"Leading Edge Trends for AI Driverless Cars"** by Dr. Lance Eliot

16. **"The Cutting Edge of AI Autonomous Cars"** by Dr. Lance Eliot

17. **"The Next Wave of AI Self-Driving Cars"** by Dr. Lance Eliot

18. **"Revolutionary Innovations of AI Driverless Cars"** by Dr. Lance Eliot

19. **"AI Self-Driving Cars Breakthroughs"** by Dr. Lance Eliot

20. **"Trailblazing Trends for AI Self-Driving Cars"** by Dr. Lance Eliot

21. **"Ingenious Strides for AI Driverless Cars"** by Dr. Lance Eliot

All of the above books are available on Amazon and at other major global booksellers.

CHAPTER 1

ELIOT FRAMEWORK FOR AI SELF-DRIVING CARS

CHAPTER 1

ELIOT FRAMEWORK FOR AI SELF-DRIVING CARS

This chapter is a core foundational aspect for understanding AI self-driving cars and I have used this same chapter in several of my other books to introduce the reader to essential elements of this field. Once you've read this chapter, you'll be prepared to read the rest of the material since the foundational essence of the components of autonomous AI driverless self-driving cars will have been established for you.

———————

When I give presentations about self-driving cars and teach classes on the topic, I have found it helpful to provide a framework around which the various key elements of self-driving cars can be understood and organized (see diagram at the end of this chapter). The framework needs to be simple enough to convey the overarching elements, but at the same time not so simple that it belies the true complexity of self-driving cars. As such, I am going to describe the framework here and try to offer in a thousand words (or more!) what the framework diagram itself intends to portray.

The core elements on the diagram are numbered for ease of reference. The numbering does not suggest any kind of prioritization of the elements. Each element is crucial. Each element has a purpose, and otherwise would not be included in the framework. For some self-driving cars, a particular element might be more important or somehow distinguished in comparison to other self-driving cars.

You could even use the framework to rate a particular self-driving car, doing so by gauging how well it performs in each of the elements of the framework. I will describe each of the elements, one at a time. After doing so, I'll discuss aspects that illustrate how the elements interact and perform during the overall effort of a self-driving car.

At the Cybernetic Self-Driving Car Institute, we use the framework to keep track of what we are working on, and how we are developing software that fills in what is needed to achieve Level 5 self-driving cars.

D-01: Sensor Capture

Let's start with the one element that often gets the most attention in the press about self-driving cars, namely, the sensory devices for a self-driving car.

On the framework, the box labeled as D-01 indicates "Sensor Capture" and refers to the processes of the self-driving car that involve collecting data from the myriad of sensors that are used for a self-driving car. The types of devices typically involved are listed, such as the use of mono cameras, stereo cameras, LIDAR devices, radar systems, ultrasonic devices, GPS, IMU, and so on.

These devices are tasked with obtaining data about the status of the self-driving car and the world around it. Some of the devices are continually providing updates, while others of the devices await an indication by the self-driving car that the device is supposed to collect data. The data might be first transformed in some fashion by the device itself, or it might instead be fed directly into the sensor capture as raw data. At that point, it might be up to the sensor capture processes to do transformations on the data. This all varies depending upon the nature of the devices being used and how the devices were designed and developed.

D-02: Sensor Fusion

Imagine that your eyeballs receive visual images, your nose receives odors, your ears receive sounds, and in essence each of your distinct sensory devices is getting some form of input. The input befits the nature of the device. Likewise, for a self-driving car, the cameras provide visual images, the radar returns radar reflections, and so on.

Each device provides the data as befits what the device does.

At some point, using the analogy to humans, you need to merge together what your eyes see, what your nose smells, what your ears hear, and piece it all together into a larger sense of what the world is all about and what is happening around you. Sensor fusion is the action of taking the singular aspects from each of the devices and putting them together into a larger puzzle.

Sensor fusion is a tough task. There are some devices that might not be working at the time of the sensor capture. Or, there might some devices that are unable to report well what they have detected. Again, using a human analogy, suppose you are in a dark room and so your eyes cannot see much. At that point, you might need to rely more so on your ears and what you hear. The same is true for a self-driving car. If the cameras are obscured due to snow and sleet, it might be that the radar can provide a greater indication of what the external conditions consist of.

In the case of a self-driving car, there can be a plethora of such sensory devices. Each is reporting what it can. Each might have its difficulties. Each might have its limitations, such as how far ahead it can detect an object. All of these limitations need to be considered during the sensor fusion task.

D-03: Virtual World Model

For humans, we presumably keep in our minds a model of the world around us when we are driving a car. In your mind, you know that the car is going at say 60 miles per hour and that you are on a freeway. You have a model in your mind that your car is surrounded by other cars, and that there are lanes to the freeway. Your model is not only based on what you can see, hear, etc., but also what you know about the nature of the world. You know that at any moment that car ahead of you can smash on its brakes, or the car behind you can ram into your car, or that the truck in the next lane might swerve into your lane.

The AI of the self-driving car needs to have a virtual world model, which it then keeps updated with whatever it is receiving from the sensor fusion, which received its input from the sensor capture and the sensory devices.

D-04: System Action Plan

By having a virtual world model, the AI of the self-driving car is able to keep track of where the car is and what is happening around the car. In addition, the AI needs to determine what to do next. Should the self-driving car hit its brakes? Should the self-driving car stay in its lane or swerve into the lane to the left? Should the self-driving car accelerate or slow down?

A system action plan needs to be prepared by the AI of the self-driving car. The action plan specifies what actions should be taken. The actions need to pertain to the status of the virtual world model. Plus, the actions need to be realizable.

This realizability means that the AI cannot just assert that the self-driving car should suddenly sprout wings and fly. Instead, the AI must be bound by whatever the self-driving car can actually do, such as coming to a halt in a distance of X feet at a speed of Y miles per hour, rather than perhaps asserting that the self-driving car come to a halt in 0 feet as though it could instantaneously come to a stop while it is in motion.

D-05: Controls Activation

The system action plan is implemented by activating the controls of the car to act according to what the plan stipulates. This might mean that the accelerator control is commanded to increase the speed of the car. Or, the steering control is commanded to turn the steering wheel 30 degrees to the left or right.

One question arises as to whether or not the controls respond as they are commanded to do. In other words, suppose the AI has commanded the accelerator to increase, but for some reason it does not do so. Or, maybe it tries to do so, but the speed of the car does not increase. The controls activation feeds back into the virtual world model, and simultaneously the virtual world model is getting updated from the sensors, the sensor capture, and the sensor fusion. This allows the AI to ascertain what has taken place as a result of the controls being commanded to take some kind of action.

By the way, please keep in mind that though the diagram seems to have a linear progression to it, the reality is that these are all aspects of the self-driving car that are happening in parallel and simultaneously. The sensors are capturing data, meanwhile the sensor fusion is taking place, meanwhile the virtual model is being updated, meanwhile the system action plan is being formulated and reformulated, meanwhile the controls are being activated.

This is the same as a human being that is driving a car. They are eyeballing the road, meanwhile they are fusing in their mind the sights, sounds, etc., meanwhile their mind is updating their model of the world around them, meanwhile they are formulating an action plan of what to do, and meanwhile they are pushing their foot onto the pedals and steering the car. In the normal course of driving a car, you are doing all of these at once. I mention this so that when you look at the diagram, you will think of the boxes as processes that are all happening at the same time, and not as though only one happens and then the next.

They are shown diagrammatically in a simplistic manner to help comprehend what is taking place. You though should also realize that they are working in parallel and simultaneous with each other. This is a tough aspect in that the inter-element communications involve latency and other aspects that must be taken into account. There can be delays in one element updating and then sharing its latest status with other elements.

D-06: Automobile & CAN

Contemporary cars use various automotive electronics and a Controller Area Network (CAN) to serve as the components that underlie the driving aspects of a car. There are Electronic Control Units (ECU's) which control subsystems of the car, such as the engine, the brakes, the doors, the windows, and so on.

The elements D-01, D-02, D-03, D-04, D-05 are layered on top of the D-06, and must be aware of the nature of what the D-06 is able to do and not do.

D-07: In-Car Commands

Humans are going to be occupants in self-driving cars. In a Level 5 self-driving car, there must be some form of communication that takes place between the humans and the self-driving car. For example, I go into a self-driving car and tell it that I want to be driven over to Disneyland, and along the way I want to stop at In-and-Out Burger. The self-driving car now parses what I've said and tries to then establish a means to carry out my wishes.

In-car commands can happen at any time during a driving journey. Though my example was about an in-car command when I first got into my self-driving car, it could be that while the self-driving car is carrying out the journey that I change my mind. Perhaps after getting stuck in traffic, I tell the self-driving car to forget about getting the burgers and just head straight over to the theme park. The self-driving car needs to be alert to in-car commands throughout the journey.

D-08: V2X Communications

We will ultimately have self-driving cars communicating with each other, doing so via V2V (Vehicle-to-Vehicle) communications. We will also have self-driving cars that communicate with the roadways and other aspects of the transportation infrastructure, doing so via V2I (Vehicle-to-Infrastructure).

The variety of ways in which a self-driving car will be communicating with other cars and infrastructure is being called V2X, whereby the letter X means whatever else we identify as something that a car should or would want to communicate with. The V2X communications will be taking place simultaneous with everything else on the diagram, and those other elements will need to incorporate whatever it gleans from those V2X communications.

D-09: Deep Learning

The use of Deep Learning permeates all other aspects of the self-driving car. The AI of the self-driving car will be using deep learning to do a better job at the systems action plan, and at the controls activation, and at the sensor fusion, and so on.

Currently, the use of artificial neural networks is the most prevalent form of deep learning. Based on large swaths of data, the neural networks attempt to "learn" from the data and therefore direct the efforts of the self-driving car accordingly.

D-10: Tactical AI

Tactical AI is the element of dealing with the moment-to-moment driving of the self-driving car. Is the self-driving car staying in its lane of the freeway? Is the car responding appropriately to the controls commands? Are the sensory devices working?

For human drivers, the tactical equivalent can be seen when you watch a novice driver such as a teenager that is first driving. They are focused on the mechanics of the driving task, keeping their eye on the road while also trying to properly control the car.

D-11: Strategic AI

The Strategic AI aspects of a self-driving car are dealing with the larger picture of what the self-driving car is trying to do. If I had asked that the self-driving car take me to Disneyland, there is an overall journey map that needs to be kept and maintained.

There is an interaction between the Strategic AI and the Tactical AI. The Strategic AI is wanting to keep on the mission of the driving, while the Tactical AI is focused on the particulars underway in the driving effort. If the Tactical AI seems to wander away from the overarching mission, the Strategic AI wants to see why and get things back on track. If the Tactical AI realizes that there is something amiss on the self-driving car, it needs to alert the Strategic AI accordingly and have an adjustment to the overarching mission that is underway.

D-12: Self-Aware AI

Very few of the self-driving cars being developed are including a Self-Aware AI element, which we at the Cybernetic Self-Driving Car Institute believe is crucial to Level 5 self-driving cars.

The Self-Aware AI element is intended to watch over itself, in the sense that the AI is making sure that the AI is working as intended. Suppose you had a human driving a car, and they were starting to drive erratically. Hopefully, their own self-awareness would make them realize they themselves are driving poorly, such as perhaps starting to fall asleep after having been driving for hours on end. If you had a passenger in the car, they might be able to alert the driver if the driver is starting to do something amiss. This is exactly what the Self-Aware

AI element tries to do, it becomes the overseer of the AI, and tries to detect when the AI has become faulty or confused, and then find ways to overcome the issue.

D-13: Economic

The economic aspects of a self-driving car are not per se a technology aspect of a self-driving car, but the economics do indeed impact the nature of a self-driving car. For example, the cost of outfitting a self-driving car with every kind of possible sensory device is prohibitive, and so choices need to be made about which devices are used. And, for those sensory devices chosen, whether they would have a full set of features or a more limited set of features.

We are going to have self-driving cars that are at the low-end of a consumer cost point, and others at the high-end of a consumer cost point. You cannot expect that the self-driving car at the low-end is going to be as robust as the one at the high-end. I realize that many of the self-driving car pundits are acting as though all self-driving cars will be the same, but they won't be. Just like anything else, we are going to have self-driving cars that have a range of capabilities. Some will be better than others. Some will be safer than others. This is the way of the real-world, and so we need to be thinking about the economics aspects when considering the nature of self-driving cars.

D-14: Societal

This component encompasses the societal aspects of AI which also impacts the technology of self-driving cars. For example, the famous Trolley Problem involves what choices should a self-driving car make when faced with life-and-death matters. If the self-driving car is about to either hit a child standing in the roadway, or instead ram into a tree at the side of the road and possibly kill the humans in the self-driving car, which choice should be made?

We need to keep in mind the societal aspects will underlie the AI of the self-driving car. Whether we are aware of it explicitly or not, the AI will have embedded into it various societal assumptions.

D-15: Innovation

I included the notion of innovation into the framework because we can anticipate that whatever a self-driving car consists of, it will continue to be innovated over time. The self-driving cars coming out in the next several years will undoubtedly be different and less innovative than the versions that come out in ten years hence, and so on.

Framework Overall

For those of you that want to learn about self-driving cars, you can potentially pick a particular element and become specialized in that aspect. Some engineers are focusing on the sensory devices. Some engineers focus on the controls activation. And so on. There are specialties in each of the elements.

Researchers are likewise specializing in various aspects. For example, there are researchers that are using Deep Learning to see how best it can be used for sensor fusion. There are other researchers that are using Deep Learning to derive good System Action Plans. Some are studying how to develop AI for the Strategic aspects of the driving task, while others are focused on the Tactical aspects.

A well-prepared all-around software developer that is involved in self-driving cars should be familiar with all of the elements, at least to the degree that they know what each element does. This is important since whatever piece of the pie that the software developer works on, they need to be knowledgeable about what the other elements are doing.

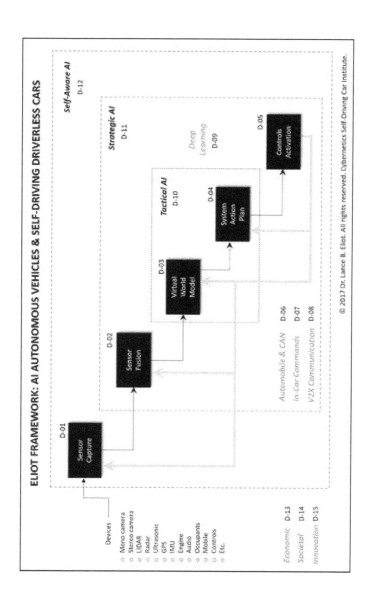

ELIOT FRAMEWORK: AI AUTONOMOUS VEHICLES & SELF-DRIVING DRIVERLESS CARS

Self-Aware AI
D-12

Strategic AI
D-11

Deep Learning
D-09

Controls Activation
D-05

Tactical AI
D-10

System Action Plan
D-04

Virtual World Model
D-03

Sensor Fusion
D-02

Sensor Capture
D-01

Devices
◇ Mono camera
◇ Stereo camera
◇ LIDAR
◇ Radar
◇ Ultrasonic
◇ GPS
◇ IMU
◇ Engine
◇ Audio
◇ Occupants
◇ Mobile
◇ Controls
◇ Etc.

Automobile & CAN   D-06
In-Car Commands   D-07
V2X Communication   D-08

Economic   D-13
Societal   D-14
Innovation D-15

CHAPTER 2

PLASTICITY
AND
AI SELF-DRIVING CARS

CHAPTER 2

PLASTICITY
AND AI SELF-DRIVING CARS

One of the most discussed advancing frontiers is plasticity.

At the forefront of the fields of cognition, biology, social ecology, physics, chemistry, computer science, neural science and studies of the brain (involving neuroplasticity), and many other disciplines, plasticity refers to the adaptability of an organism or equivalent to be able to change and adapt to its environment or habitat.

There have been recently reported cases of phenotypic plasticity in certain kinds of toads, roundworms, lizards, and other creatures that has caused some evolutionary biologists to take a second look at Darwin's theories of evolution. We all know from our science and history classes that Darwin shook-up the world when he proposed his theory that survival of the fittest implies that organisms don't just suddenly change their core traits to fit to the environment.

Instead, there are presumed random genetic mutations that change a trait and for which if the changed trait is a better fit to the environment, the mutated creature will tend to survive and procreate in that environment. As the mutated creature continues to survive and procreate over some number of generations, more so than the unmutated similar organisms that are a lesser fit to the environment, the mutated one becomes prevalent and the other one(s) gradually diminish or die off.

Prior to Darwin, there was some naturalists such as Jean-Baptiste Lamarck that postulated it might be possible for evolutionary change to happen in the midst of a single lifetime and not need to work itself out over multiple generations. It was Darwin and others of his ilk that asserted that the "single lifetime" approach was essentially infeasible and unlikely, and that the notion of a multi-generational playout was seemingly more logical and likely.

Let's consider the use case of a giraffe and its neck.

Suppose we have a bunch of giraffes and they all have long necks. These long necks allow them to eat leaves from acacia trees and they need to consume around 75 pounds of such food per day to remain hunger-free. The acacia trees have thorns that tend to prevent other animals from eating the leaves, especially at the lower realms of the tree, and the long necks of the giraffe gives it an environmental advantage since they can reach higher up in the tree.

Using Darwin's theory of the world, let's pretend that we have a giraffe that gets born with a much shorter neck. Assume it is a random mutation of the neck gene of giraffes. What will happen to the shorter necked giraffe? It might or might not survive in its lifetime, perhaps starving off because it cannot reach the higher plentiful and available leaves of the acacia tree.

Let's imagine that this shorter neck giraffe manages to mate during its lifetime and the offspring carry the shorter neck gene and are once again shorter necked giraffes. Presumably, the long neck giraffes are still doing fine and living and procreating, meanwhile this new version of a giraffe, the short neck version, will be struggling to survive. It could be that the shorter neck is such a lousy fit to the environment that eventually all those with the mutated gene die off and any of their procreated offspring die off too. No more shorter neck giraffes, until or if another mutated gene randomness reoccurs.

So far, so good, in terms of conforming to what Darwin's theories expound.

Somehow, let's pretend that the acacia tree suddenly stops producing leaves high-up and instead only does so nearer the lower portions of the tree.

The environment has changed!

Now, the longer necked giraffes find themselves in a bit of a pickle. They need to dip further down and try to eat those luscious leaves. But, imagine that it is very hard for them to do so. Furthermore, in the act of bending down like this, they no longer keep their eye on predators. This is a double whammy for the long-necked giraffes. They are having difficulty getting sufficient food for survival, plus, predators now are able to sneak-up more so on them and cull the herds of giraffes.

Meanwhile, let's go ahead and revisit our random mutated gene that produces short necked giraffes. A short-necked giraffe is born based on the randomly mutated neck gene. It is well suited to eat the leaves lower down on the acacia tree. It is more well suited to see predators, at least now more than the bending over long-necked giraffes. The short-necked giraffe is more likely to live its lifetime and procreate, and the offspring will enjoy the same kind of advantage in this changed environment.

Eventually, presumably inexorably, the long-necked giraffes are going to thin out and die off, while the short-necked giraffes will be a better fit to the environmental change that occurred and thrive.

As an aside, let's all agree that this is a rather simplistic view of evolutionary aspects since we might be more likely to have a multitude of environmental changes taking place simultaneously, all of which can both aid and possibly undermine the status of giraffes (both long-necked and short-necked) in various ways, plus we might also expect that other kinds of mutations are randomly occurring that can hinder or help survival (maybe long-legs versus short-legs, maybe shape eyes versus less-focused eyes, and so on).

In any case, here's a question for you to ponder: Can a long-necked giraffe within its own lifetime suddenly "mutate" into becoming a short-necked giraffe in order to better fit to this changed environment about the nature of the acacia trees?

I'd wager that most if not all of us would assert that the long-necked giraffe cannot suddenly and spontaneously mutate during its own lifetime. It is stuck with the genes that it has. Tough luck. It might produce offspring having a random mutation toward a shorter neck, though this would presumably be purely by random chance and not by something that the adult did to cause it to occur (unless perhaps it mated with the shorter-neck giraffes under some belief this would be a good path to offspring survival or maybe by simply being attracted to the now hunger-free shorter necked blossoming giraffes). The adult long-neck though is doomed to live a life of a long-neck and might as well party to the very bitter end.

What has caused a bit of a stir in the standard Darwin theory is that there seem to be some animals that defy the "you cannot change in your lifetime" provision. In a particular species of toads, the spadefoot toad, when they produce their itty-bitty tadpoles, apparently the offspring tend toward eating algae, they are calm and mild mannered tadpoles, and are small-jawed. It is reported that if the water body the tadpoles are in contains let's say fairy shrimp, some of the tadpoles "transform" into aggressively devouring carnivores and display bulging jaws along with a fierce demeanor.

So, when the environment is the normal and expected calm pool of water and there is nothing carnivorous to eat, the tadpoles are relatively docile algae eaters. If instead the water contains large crustaceans such as shrimps, a change in their normal environment, some of those same tadpoles become intense meat eaters that will take on any comers, which gives them an added advantage in that environment.

It would almost be as though a long-necked giraffe could suddenly transform into a short-necked giraffe, during its lifetime, in order to adjust to the changed environment about the acacia trees. Doing so would presumably make it a better fit to the changed environment.

This would in turn give it better odds of survival. If this same aspect was innate in the transformational giraffe, it could pass it along to its offspring which then would also be better suited to the changed environment.

One explanation about the transforming tadpoles and other such creatures has been the suggestion that there might be a plasticity element involved in this. The plasticity theory keeps Darwin's theory intact. Some are referring to the "discovery" or more like the scientific realization and emergence of plasticity as a sign that maybe there is a plasticity-first form of evolution.

Let's consider how plasticity comes to play.

Suppose that some of the long-necked giraffes have a hidden trait that they've not yet had cause to consider using. The hidden trait is that they can bend their necks down relatively easily and do so while still keeping their eyes up and able to spot predators. The more traditional long-necked giraffes don't have this innate trait.

All of the long-necked giraffes lived together in harmony and did not realize that some of them had this bending neck capability that was baked into their genetics and could be used during their lifetime, if they wished to do so. Let's assume there was no outwardly sign that some of the giraffes had this hidden trait. The special trait giraffes blended in naturally with the rest of their long-necked friends and colleagues.

When the environment changes, involving the acacia trees leaves, all of a sudden, the long-necked giraffes that have this hidden trait are able to immediately and readily adjust to the environmental change. From an observer's perspective, we might think that some of these giraffes have magically "transformed" nearly overnight, doing so in the midst of their own lifetime. Instead, what's really happened is that there were some giraffes that happened to have this otherwise hidden trait and now there was value in them employing it for their survival and giving us as humans the perchance to witness it.

This is one possible explanation for the tadpoles too. Perhaps they have a dominant trait built-in of being polite and vegans, but they also have a hidden trait of being fierce carnivores when needed. Upon experiencing an environment for which the hidden trait has value, some of those tadpoles display the hidden trait. For a human observing the tadpoles, it seems strange and unpredictable that some would "transform" in their given lifetime, when in fact it is simply that they've been triggered to use a hidden talent that was there all along.

It could be that there are even more such hidden traits in that subset of the long-necked giraffes and the tadpoles. We might just not know those hidden traits are there because we've not seen them deployed.

In fact, it could be that the subset of giraffes or tadpoles have not just specific hidden traits of varying kinds, but maybe they have an overarching plasticity trait. The plasticity trait governs their ability to deploy other hidden traits and aids and abets the emergence of those hidden traits.

In that case, the environment can change in a myriad of ways, and yet those giraffes that carry the plasticity trait are going to have better odds of coping with the changed environment, even during a specific lifetime in which the environmental change emerges. This plasticity trait might end-up making them especially fit to survive and also therefore have a solid chance of producing offspring carrying the trait.

We can recast the topic plasticity into another realm, namely the nature of the human brain. The human brain appears to be capable of changing and adapting, doing so in neurobiological ways and also in more abstract cognitive ways. There is a continual effort underway of forming and adapting amongst the synapses that connect the neurons in the brain, which we assume is the brain's way of reorganizing itself and learning and changing.

For those of you versed in Machine Learning (ML) and Deep Learning (DL), you likely know that right now most of the computational models used for crafting Artificial Neural Networks (ANN or sometimes shortened to just NN) are typically rigid and locked-in once they've been initially trained.

You toss a million pictures of cats at a deep learning system and once you are satisfied that it seems to pattern-match relatively well in terms of discerning what a cat looks like, doing so by having adjusted automatically or semi-automatically the number of artificial neurons, the layers, and their connections, you then will tend to deploy that deep learning system "as is" and let it do its cat identification magic.

The finalized or deployed version takes as input a new image that might or might not contain a cat in it and ascertains to some probability that there is a cat in the picture or not in the picture and indicates where the cat seems to be.

In today's deep learning implementations, it is rare that you would have the deployed artificial neural network change and adapt while it is deployed. You more likely might do a retraining if you believe that the deep learning needs further depth or refinement. This would be done in a controlled setting usually, and not in a live environment.

If we are all ultimately aiming to have "true" deep learning and do so by properly modelling and mimicking how the human brain really works, it would seem like we ought to be building into our Machine Learning and our artificial neural networks the plasticity capability that real brains seem to have. In the real-world, the brain is continually changing and adapting, and so should our deep learning models.

What does this have to do with AI self-driving cars?

At the Cybernetic AI Self-Driving Car Institute, we are developing AI software for self-driving cars. One aspect that we are building into our AI systems is a form of DL neuronal plasticity. We believe it is essential as an element for advancing AI and likewise ML and deep learning capabilities of computing.

Allow me to elaborate.

I'd like to first clarify and introduce the notion that there are varying levels of AI self-driving cars. The topmost level is considered Level 5. A Level 5 self-driving car is one that is being driven by the AI and there is no human driver involved. For the design of Level 5 self-driving cars, the auto makers are even removing the gas pedal, brake pedal, and steering wheel, since those are contraptions used by human drivers. The Level 5 self-driving car is not being driven by a human and nor is there an expectation that a human driver will be present in the self-driving car. It's all on the shoulders of the AI to drive the car.

For self-driving cars less than a Level 5, there must be a human driver present in the car. The human driver is currently considered the responsible party for the acts of the car. The AI and the human driver are co-sharing the driving task. In spite of this co-sharing, the human is supposed to remain fully immersed into the driving task and be ready at all times to perform the driving task. I've repeatedly warned about the dangers of this co-sharing arrangement and predicted it will produce many untoward results.

Let's focus herein on the true Level 5 self-driving car. Much of the comments apply to the less than Level 5 self-driving cars too, but the fully autonomous AI self-driving car will receive the most attention in this discussion.

Here's the usual steps involved in the AI driving task:
- Sensor data collection and interpretation
- Sensor fusion
- Virtual world model updating
- AI action planning
- Car controls command issuance

Another key aspect of AI self-driving cars is that they will be driving on our roadways in the midst of human driven cars too. There are some pundits of AI self-driving cars that continually refer to a utopian world in which there are only AI self-driving cars on the public roads. Currently there are about 250+ million conventional cars in the United States alone, and those cars are not going to magically disappear or become true Level 5 AI self-driving cars overnight.

Indeed, the use of human driven cars will last for many years, likely many decades, and the advent of AI self-driving cars will occur while there are still human driven cars on the roads. This is a crucial point since this means that the AI of self-driving cars needs to be able to contend with not just other AI self-driving cars, but also contend with human driven cars. It is easy to envision a simplistic and rather unrealistic world in which all AI self-driving cars are politely interacting with each other and being civil about roadway interactions. That's not what is going to be happening for the foreseeable future. AI self-driving cars and human driven cars will need to be able to cope with each other.

Returning to the topic of plasticity, consider for a moment that by-and-large the auto makers and tech firms are currently making use of Machine Learning and DL for AI self-driving cars in a rather narrow portion of the "stack" or spectrum of driving tasks that need to be performed by the AI system.

In terms of a driving tasks stack, by-and-large today's use of ML in self-driving cars is primarily focused at the sensors level of the AI self-driving car automation. There is much less effort underway in terms of using ML and DL for the sensor fusion portion and even less so for the AI action planning and virtual world model updating and analysis.

This initial preoccupation with the sensory data makes sense. The multitude of sensors and their data capture provides an exquisitely rich source of voluminous data and it is relatively easy to come by. Furthermore, vast swaths of data is customarily needed to best make use of today's ML and DL capabilities, it is their lifeblood, so to speak. For example, feed a ton of images of street signs into a convolutional neural network and you are ultimately presumably going to be able to have a handy and relatively accurate visualization detector of street signs when an AI self-driving car is on-the-road.

Human drivers are particularly adept at visually scanning the surroundings of a car and being able to detect and decipher what they see. Those trees over there aren't important, but that parked car that appears to be pulling out into the street is important.

Those pedestrians standing at the curb and waiting to cross the street, they are important, but that dog on a leash that is tied-up to the bike rack near the front door of that store is not important. By importance, I mean to suggest that the driver is able to discern what those various objects are, and whether or not they pertain to the driving task at-hand.

Numerous efforts are taking place at improving the ability to use ML and DL to examine visual images that are captured via the camera and video recording devices on AI self-driving cars. Likewise, via the use of ML and DL, patterns can be found in the radar collected data, the LIDAR collected data, the ultrasonic collected data, and other such data sources. An AI self-driving car needs to figure out what is surrounding the car and then make use of that informed "awareness" to decide what actions the self-driving car should undertake.

A self-driving car that cannot detect its surroundings adequately is going to fail. Didn't notice that pedestrian crossing the street in front of the self-driving car, bam, down goes the pedestrian. Didn't detect that car up ahead that is veering into the lane of the self-driving car, crash, the two cars hit each other. Fundamentally, the AI system needs to have sufficient sensory capabilities to figure out what objects are nearby and where those objects are, along with where they might be going.

It takes though a lot more than just seeing or detecting something to be able to drive a car.

Even if you see the pedestrian crossing the street, you need to put two-plus-two together and realize that there is a chance that the path of the car is going to intersect with the pedestrian, and the car will end-up harming the person. Upon that realization, you then need to try and decide what to do. Should you slow down? Should you swerve away from the pedestrian? Radically hit the brakes? Maybe speed-up?

The AI action planning portion of the driving task is when the driving behavior becomes sacrosanct.

The sensors have provided their data and the sensor interpretations indicate what objects are out there. The sensor fusion has tried to meld together the sensor data and interpretations into a consistent overall indication of the surroundings. The virtual world model indicates the surroundings, the objects, and the speed and direction and other aspects of those objects. It is now up to the AI action planner element to do what human drivers seem to be able to do, assess the situation and decide what next action is best for the driving of the car.

For modeling of human driving behavior, most of the auto makers and tech firms have to-date been using a rather rudimentary and programmatic approach to having the AI action planner perform its function. They have crudely been programming the more simplistic aspects of human driving decisions into the AI system. If there is a pedestrian in the road up ahead, and if the self-driving car is going to intersect, first calculate if the self-driving car can stop in time. If stopping in time is not feasible then consider a swerving action. And so on.

The AI action planner element:

- Currently tends to be rigid and programmatically depicted, rather than being fluid and based on Machine Learning or Deep Learning aspects derived from human driver behaviors,

- Generally, tends to be based on simplistic hard-coded rules by the AI-developers about how driving is supposed to happen versus based on real-world data of how drivers actually drive

- Will be a key and severe limitation or constraint toward achieving true Level 5 self-driving cars since it will inhibit or undermine the AI to be able to step-up to the myriad of innumerable ill-defined driving situations that will be encountered on public roadways.

Our AI development effort involves using a repository of driving behavior templates, traits as it were, which are based on human driving experiences, and as pattern-matched via the use of Machine Learning and Deep Learning.

In essence, apply the same kind of ML/DL techniques to the detection of objects in the sensory data, but use it for the formulation of driving behaviors based on voluminous driving behavior data rather than sensory images data, and then apply those driving behavior traits to roadway situations as they arise while driving the car.

In addition, this use of ML and DL is not just as a pre-training and pre-deployment kind of operation. Instead, the ML and DL continues while the AI is driving the self-driving car. Learning on the fly is considered an equally valid avenue of learning. Admittedly, in the case of driving a car, some rather significant "guardrails" need to be embodied into the AI system to prevent it from learning "the wrong thing" and taking an untoward driving action accordingly.

Humans of course continue to learn about driving when they are driving a car.

Each time you get behind the wheel, there is an opportunity to learn something new about driving. That being said, I realize that most of us as seasoned-drivers have driven sufficiently that it becomes less and less likely that we'll learn something new about driving when we get on the road. The already robust base of experience at driving becomes extensive enough that most of the daily driving situations that arise have all been seen before, and our minds already learnt how to cope with the situation.

There is a plasticity in your driving behavior, which makes sense when you contemplate the matter.

When you start to drive as a novice in your teenage years, you have a great deal of plasticity since you are rapidly trying to absorb a swirl of driving tactics and strategies, along with devising tactics and strategies that aren't otherwise already brought to your attention. You are like a nearly empty mental vessel about driving when you first learn to drive, though you certainly already have a great deal of supporting richness of knowledge such as how streets work, how pedestrians work, how cars go, etc. I mention this because I don't want to imply that you are empty-headed when you learn to drive – there's plenty of important stuff that's already in your noggin.

There is "supervised" leaning in which someone explains to you a driving tactic or strategy, such as a driving instructor or perhaps a caring parent that is helping you learn to drive. And there is "unsupervised" learning that involves your own efforts to glean what is happening as you drive, and not only cope with the moment, but also turn the moment into a permanent member of your driving behavior (as a newly formed or revised trait or template) that will become part of your overall mental repository of driving templates or traits.

Let's consider two use cases. The first will involve a novice teenage driver. The second use case will involve a seasoned driver.

I was helping my teenage children learn to drive, which is both an honor and somewhat scary. You realize rather quickly that there is little you can do from the front passenger seat if your offspring happens to make a wrong move while driving the car.

When I first learned to drive, my high school had specially equipped cars that had dual controls, one for the teenager at the driver's wheel and another set of controls for the driving instructor sitting in the front passenger seat. Everyone going to the high school was able to take a beginner's driving course. This made things somewhat easier for parents at the time.

In terms of the driving instructor, I'm not suggesting that the dual controls made life any easier for that teacher, since I can only imagine what his or her life must have been like to work with teenagers all day long in a car that can get into life-or-death predicaments, regardless of the instructor also having access to the driving controls. Forever bless those instructors!

Anyway, after having practiced on local streets with my children driving, it seemed time to try using a freeway. Up until that moment, the fastest we had the car going was maybe 45-50 miles per hour. Now, once we got onto the freeway, it would be more like 60-70 miles per hour. A lot faster than 40-50 mph, even though I realize you might argue it is only "a few mph faster" (it is exponentially higher, on a frightening perceptual scale, I assert). There's a lot less time to take needed actions. A lot higher chance of things going awry. Fatherly love made me take the chance.

When they reached the on-ramp, they each drove up the ramp and tried to enter into the freeway traffic at the top speed they had already gotten used to, namely the 45-50 miles per hour. I had chosen a time of day when there wasn't much traffic on the freeway so that we'd be able to drive along steadily and not simply be mired in the usual Southern California bumper-to-bumper snarl. As such, the prevailing traffic was easily doing 65 to perhaps 75 miles per hour (yes, those higher speeds exceed the legal speed limit, but the speed limit is considered more of a suggestion than an imperative here).

I realized immediately that we were going to enter into traffic at a much lower speed than the prevailing traffic. I'm sure you've done this before or seen it done by others. The driving problem this creates is that you might end-up merging in front of cars that will have to pump their brakes to keep from ramming into you, or you might cause other cars to have to do a dance trying to get away from the slower going car, all of which could cause a cascade of crashes.

I urged that they push down hard on the accelerator pedal and give us a flash of speed to try and match the prevailing traffic speed. I'm sure that some teenagers would love to do this, willingly and gladly putting the pedal to the floor. My children were more conservative and cautious, thankfully so, and I had to really emphasize the need for speed. Fortunately, we made it okay and nothing untoward happened.

The story might end there, except for the valuable insight it provides about driving behavior and the learning of driving tactics and strategies.

Shortly after that one incident, we ended-up in other situations whereby the need to match the speed of prevailing traffic arose. For example, as they tried to make it to the desired exit ramp, they were in a faster lane and had to slightly decrease their speed to match the cars in the slower lane that led to the exit ramp. I could see them concentrating on what to do and then adjusting their speed accordingly. When we got off the freeway, the off-ramp was a fast turn directly into a busy highway, and they once again had a look of concentration and matched their speed to the prevailing traffic.

They each had adapted to the "new" environmental conditions that involved as a potential "solution" a speed-matching approach (the word "new" in this case refers to their first time driving on a freeway and at predominant high speeds).

Based on the one instance of coming onto the freeway, they had each crafted on-their-own a mental template or trait that imbued them with the driving tactic that when the circumstances warranted it, they considered a "matching the speed" maneuver. Notice that I had not said to them "whenever the situation arises, such as getting onto the freeway or getting off the freeway, adjust your speed to the prevailing traffic." They devised this notion on their own, merely by my impetus to them to speed-up at the first occasion.

You could say that they learned in a somewhat supervisory fashion, since I did give them a tip or hint and it was presumably my nudge that started them toward the tactic.

It is also interesting that they could have gained a narrower lesson learned in that suppose their thought was that if you need to go faster then go faster. In the aspect of trying to later on get to the exit ramp, they had to actually go slower to match to the slower moving traffic. If the hard-coded rule was go faster, it would not have lent itself to the broader notion of matching the prevailing speed.

These human drivers learned an important driving behavior, which I'm sure became part of their overall driving lexicon.

Did they have to drive a thousand times on thousands of on-ramps to derive the lesson learned? No. I mention this because the prevailing approach to Machine Learning and Deep Learning requires humungous volumes of data. Presumably, the only way a conventional ML or DL could have devised the match-the-speed template or trait would be to have had thousands or maybe hundreds of thousands of traffic flows data to try and pattern onto.

We don't think that's needed for doing driving behavior adaptability for an AI system. It helps to have such data, but it isn't a prerequisite and nor is it the only way to learn.

One thing the kids did have was plasticity. They came onto that on-ramp with a limited set of prior driving experiences. They had to be prepared to change, in the sense of perhaps learning something new or adjusting things that they had earlier learned. They were being confronted with a new environment, a new driving environment from their perspective. It would require honing new driving skills to survive. And, they needed to do so in real-time, in the real-world, in a situation involving real cars and real life-or-death matters at-hand. Adapt or die, I suppose one might say.

The next use case involves a seasoned driver. Me. I'm going to describe it rather briefly here since I've already extensively covered the use case in my other writings.

As a seasoned driver, there is not much that I could likely learn anew about driving, though there are always those moments whereby a driving tactic or strategy can be further refined or extended.

You never know when you might get a chance to learn something new for your driving repertoire. Some seasoned drivers that I know have never driven in snow, and thus upon their first encounter with trying to drive a car on snow, they might rediscover the joys of learning something new (to them) about the driving task.

In any case, on my daily commute to work, I drive in the hustle and bustle of Southern California traffic.

Here, especially it seems, everyone wants to get to where they are going in the fastest possible way. For some drivers, they believe that by riding the bumper of the car ahead of them, it is going to magically make things go faster. I've debunked this notion overall by examining traffic data and simulations and analyzing it to showcase that this driving tactic not only at times will not work as intended, it can backfire and make traffic go slower, causing at times for the driver to take even longer to get to where they are going. They ironically worsen traffic and make it go slower, in spite of their (false) belief that they are going to speed things up.

Nonetheless, the average pushy driver thinks (rightly or wrongly) that they will get traffic to go faster if they "push" the car ahead of them by coming right up to the back of the car and motivate the driver therein to go faster (or, presumably, get that driver out of the way so that the "faster" driver behind them can get further ahead).

I am accustomed to this driving behavior.

So much so that I anticipate it. I know that a high percentage of drivers here in Los Angeles are going to ride on my tail. No matter what speed I might be going, even if going over the speed limit, these other speed demons are going to go to the bumper. Unfortunately, this kind of driving behavior can have adverse consequences. For example, the driver being tailed now has to be watchful of trying to use their brakes, since the car behind them has little buffer distance to also slow down or stop.

I realize that some drivers figure that if the driver behind them is stupid and doesn't allocate enough buffer distance, it is the fault of that driver and nothing else is to be done. For me, and for any truly defensive oriented driver, it is crucial to not simply let other "dumber" drivers dictate our options, but it is best to consider how to drive in a manner that takes into account those other drivers and their driving foibles.

After years of my adapting to this driving environment of pushy drivers that constantly are riding on the bumpers of other cars, it had become ingrained in my driving style. My adaptations included numerous driving tactics. For example, you can avoid a pushy driver by potentially spotting them in your rearview mirror long before they get behind your car, in which case, you can then get into a position that will likely preclude them from getting directly behind you, if you plan out the movement of nearby cars and the maneuvering of your car in a chess-like way. And so on.

What makes this driving behavior template or trait of interest herein is that when I recently took a vacation and went to a location that did not have these same kinds of pushy drivers (or, had them but to a much lesser degree), my driving continued as though I was still in the same environment. Each car that I saw coming along, my assumption was that this was most likely a pushy driver, regardless of how they were actually driving, and I silently and subliminally was invoking my pushy-driver control tactics.

This aspect that I fell into is a mental trap known as prevalence-induced behavior.

Conclusion

I'll tie together the giraffes and the tadpoles with the aspects of driving and driving behaviors. They all interrelate by the matter of considering what kinds of traits we have, some of which are innate, some of which are learned, along with the plasticity of being able to change and adapt to our environment. If Darwin were still here, I'm sure he'd be interested in this topic too.

To further advance AI, I'd wager that we'll need to make progress on Machine Learning and Deep Learning that will incorporate plasticity. We need to be able to construct artificial neural networks that can change and adapt and adjust as the environment changes, in real-time, in a real-world context, and essentially on-their-own as we've hopefully imbued them with the capabilities to do so.

In that sense, we should all be aiming to have artificial neuroplasticity, which, since real neuroplasticity occurs in the brain, we likely will need to do something likewise in the computer if we are going to reach AI brain-like capabilities.

For driving purposes, the AI action planning is where the crux of driving and driving behaviors resides. Being able to see and sense the driving environment provides the so-called table stakes for playing the self-driving AI game, but to really succeed in AI self-driving cars will require the AI to be able to drive with driving behaviors, ones that are honed and pre-tuned, and others that will arise as the driving situation emerges and the driving environment changes (as perceived by the AI).

If those tadpoles have the ability to change how they act and look, doing so after sensing the environmental conditions that warrant a change, and presumably bringing forth some kind of latent traits that can be triggered and showcase the plasticity of these toads, I'm voting that we can do the same kind of thing with driver behavior templates and traits, for which the AI self-driving car would use and refine, based on the driving environment and the plasticity that we've built into the AI. Score one for the humans and let's show those malleable tadpoles what we can really achieve.

CHAPTER 3
NIMBY VS. YIMBY
AND
AI SELF-DRIVING CARS

CHAPTER 3

NIMBY VS. YIMBY
AND
AI SELF-DRIVING CARS

NIMBY. You've likely heard or seen the acronym before. Not In My Backyard (NIMBY). That's what some people say when there is something they believe to be untoward that is potentially going to be situated near to them. It can be used in a rather literal sense, such as next door to your home there is going to be a homeless shelter put in place and you object to the shelter being located in that particular spot. Or, it could be that the homeless shelter will be somewhere in your neighborhood and you likewise believe it should not be located that close to where you live.

Keep in mind that you might actually welcome the notion of having homeless shelters and you have no overarching objection to those facilities. Your carp is that it is being located in a place that you believe is inappropriate. You might have compelling reasons for your belief. Maybe there are school children that are in your neighborhood and you are worried about their safety as it relates to having a nearby homeless shelter. Etc.

Often times, people will indicate they favor something overall, and it is the specific placement that concerns them.

A frequent retort to that involves the suggestion that the person does not want to bear having the aspect near to them but seems willing to have someone else have to deal with the matter.

When respondent's fill-in a poll or survey and say they are in favor of something, their response can change dramatically if the question indicates that the something will be in their backyard, so to speak.

Is it being two-faced or perhaps hypocritical to indicate that you favor something but not in your own backyard? That's the claim that some make against those that say yes to something and yet refuse to have it near to them. This though seems a bit at times over-the-top because suppose the person genuinely believes that the matter should be dealt with and has other bona fide alternative suggestions about its placement. Suppose they advocated that the homeless shelter should be built in an area more accommodating for the needs of the homeless, and thus it is not just that the person doesn't want it in their own backyard and could be that there are logical reasons to place it someplace else.

This is not to say that there aren't some that are indeed perhaps being two-faced at times. It could be that there is not a particularly valid justification to refuse having the matter located near to them. They maybe fabricate a reason for their viewpoint on the matter. They might even opt to avoid offering any rationale per se and instead just flatly insist that they don't want the aspect located near to them.

The debate about locating something can be a mixture of rational discussion and heated emotion. This combination is akin to mixing gasoline and diesel fuel, creating an explosive result.

You might have some proponents of locating a matter in your neighborhood that have impeccably logical reasons to do so, and you might oppose it on purely emotional terms. Or, maybe the proponents are the ones with the emotionally laden basis and you are the one with the rationally logical reasons against it.

Most times, it is likely that both sides have a combined mixture, namely they will vacillate between offering logical reasons and emotional responses, and it can be hard to separate those two elements when having a discussion or debate on the matter.

Consider the rise of nuclear power plants. When nuclear power plants were first devised, there were many locales that welcomed having one built in their vicinity. It was considered by some to be a modernistic element of society. It offered the creation of jobs in the locale where it was being placed. It was promoted as reducing energy costs and would therefore provide monetary savings to those that tapped into the power generated. And so on.

Eventually, there were various issues that arose about nuclear power plants and it became a kind of pariah to have one in your locale. Nuclear power plants became the butt of jokes about how poorly run they were and the dangers they created. Some locales that had one were desperate to try and close down that nuclear power plant. Other locations that were approached to have a nuclear power plant built in their vicinity were quick to say NIMBY.

This illustrates too that the NIMBY is not confined to just being located next door to you or in your neighborhood and can include a much larger geographic factor. The NIMBY might be that you don't want something to be placed in your city, or maybe not in your county, or perhaps not in your state, and it could be that you enlarge the scope to not being in your country. I don't want the Widget factory anywhere in the United States, you might contend, whereby the Widget factory is something you consider so untoward that you don't want it within the borders of your country.

Another example would be nuclear waste. Some people might say that there should not be nuclear waste stored anywhere in their country. Others might be Okay with storing it someplace in their country, but not anywhere physically close to them.

The item involved does not necessarily need to be stationary.

In the case of nuclear waste, suppose there is a train that takes the nuclear waste from point A to point B. During transit, the train is going to come through your city. Even though it might only be inside the confines of your city for presumably a short period of time, you might still have a NIMBY. You are maybe worried that the radiation could harm locals, or perhaps the train might derail and create a nuclear waste disaster in your town.

If we took a poll of the members of your town, it might not necessarily show that everyone feels the same way about the matter. There are likely to be some people that will be quite strongly voiced about the matter. They might be advocates in favor of the aspect and be outspoken for it, while there might be others that are on the opposite side and outspoken in opposition to it. Likely there will be some people that are on-the-fence and say they are open to learning more about it. There are bound to be some people that claim they don't care either way and don't want to get immersed in it at all.

I mention this to clarify that the NIMBY can be the viewpoint of just one person or it can be a group of people. Furthermore, the NIMBY might not be unanimous amongst a group of people, depending upon how we choose the group. If we ask just those that are in favor of the matter, presumably the vote would be unanimous in favor of it. If we ask the entire town, we'd perhaps have a segment that was the group in favor of it, we'd have the segment that was vitriolically opposed, we'd have the on-the-fence segment, and we'd have the don't care segment.

All of these perceptions can change over time.

Consider Amazon's efforts to find a place to put their second headquarters, often referred to as the HQ2. In some communities, there were advocates relishing that the HQ2 be placed in their city or town. There were some members of that city or town that were likely opposed, and others in the middle, and some that said they didn't care either way.

Any of those positions on the matter were at times fluid and apt to change. For some locales, they at first welcomed the HQ2 as a potential newcomer, and then later changed their minds and opposed it. That's how these things often go. There is not a fixed-in-stone perspective and instead it will at times shift or transform as to whether people favor or disfavor a matter.

YIMBY. You might not have seen or heard YIMBY, and it certainly is less well-known than NIMBY. YIMBY means Yes In My Backyard. It is considered the counterpart to the NIMBY. On one side of the location issues you might have those saying keep the matter out of their locale, those are the NIMBY's, and you might have equally strong advocates that are insisting the matter should be in the locale, the YIMBY's.

Note that YIMBY is not the only acronym used to refer to those that want something in their backyard, but it seems to be on its way to becoming the most prevalent.

How do people form their NIMBY or YIMBY perspectives?

Some people might carefully research a matter, studying it quite closely. They might seek the viewpoints of established experts in the matter. Their NIMBY or YIMBY might be based on gobs of rationale and they can spit out the twenty reasons for their position.

There are others that might have heard second-hand about the topic or marginally know much about it, but they too might form NIMBY or YIMBY positions, albeit not quite as well articulated and supported. There are some that might go with their gut. There are some that might figure that if Joe or Samantha are NIMBY or YIMBY, and if they believe in that person, they might simply form their own viewpoint based on a sense of "trust" in that other person's position.

The information that either supports the NIMBY or the YIMBY positions can be widely available and highly accurate. Or, it can be sparsely available and at times riddled with flaws. There can be disinformation that distorts the matter and creates confusion about what is "true" versus what is "false" regarding the matter. There can be a lack of information on the topic, which can create a vacuum into which fake information can arise.

You can become saturated with information that seems completely sensible and valid for both sides of the NIMBY and the YIMBY debate, but it is voluminous, maybe highly technical and somewhat unreadable or not readily digested. It can be overwhelming. You might not know how to sort out what seems viable in the morass.

The difficulty can be further exacerbated by the classic dueling-experts. This involves having one seemingly fully qualified expert that offers a viewpoint that seems to completely support the NIMBY, and yet have another equally fully-qualified expert that takes the side that seems to support the YIMBY. How are you to decide when two renowned experts are diametrically opposed to each other's claims or rational?

Local leaders will often have a stake in the matter too. Perhaps the item to be potentially located in your town or city is considered good for the town or city, and a local leader therefore believes it will have tremendous benefits for the community. They might believe this in their heart and soul. They might also see this as a means to extend or expand their local leadership aims. Of course, there are local leaders that might be on the opposite side too, namely they believe earnestly in their heart and soul that the matter would be damaging or undermining to the community.

In that sense, there is at times a kind of ROI (Return on Investment) analysis that often occurs. This could involve trying to identify all of the benefits, perhaps trying to quantify them in terms of how it might improve lives or make money or have other desirable outcomes. This then might be balanced by the potential costs. Perhaps the matter poses risks for the community. Maybe it would require an expenditure of monies and there is concern that the matter won't pencil out as a profitable choice.

The cost-benefit analysis could be extensively undertaken and involve lots of surveys and include notable experts that weigh-in on the matter. Sometimes there is no particular overt cost-benefit analysis undertaken and the matter is more one of viewed in disconnected bits and pieces. There might be conjecture rather than solid analysis. That's not to suggest that a cost-benefit analysis could not also be spiked or biased, which could indeed happen. Doing a comprehensive cost-benefit analysis can be costly in itself and thus the effort to do so needs to be considered accordingly.

What does this have to do with AI self-driving cars?

At the Cybernetic AI Self-Driving Car Institute, we are developing AI software for self-driving cars. There are some communities that are eager to have AI self-driving cars get underway on their public streets, those are the YIMBY's. There are other communities that aren't yet in the mindset of the YIMBY, and vary from being NIMBY's to perhaps the let's wait-and-see types. There are some communities that aren't even in the game as yet, so to speak, in that so far, there's not been any auto maker or tech firm with AI self-driving cars that has approached that community about their interest in allowing AI self-driving cars on their roadways.

Let's consider the various aspects about this YIMBY versus NIMBY in terms of the advent of AI self-driving cars.

I'd like to first clarify and introduce the notion that there are varying levels of AI self-driving cars. The topmost level is considered Level 5. A Level 5 self-driving car is one that is being driven by the AI and there is no human driver involved. For the design of Level 5 self-driving cars, the auto makers are even removing the gas pedal, brake pedal, and steering wheel, since those are contraptions used by human drivers. The Level 5 self-driving car is not being driven by a human and nor is there an expectation that a human driver will be present in the self-driving car. It's all on the shoulders of the AI to drive the car.

For self-driving cars less than a Level 5, there must be a human driver present in the car. The human driver is currently considered the responsible party for the acts of the car. The AI and the human driver are co-sharing the driving task. In spite of this co-sharing, the human is supposed to remain fully immersed into the driving task and be ready at all times to perform the driving task. I've repeatedly warned about the dangers of this co-sharing arrangement and predicted it will produce many untoward results.

Let's focus herein on the true Level 5 self-driving car. Much of the comments apply to the less than Level 5 self-driving cars too, but the fully autonomous AI self-driving car will receive the most attention in this discussion.

Here's the usual steps involved in the AI driving task:
- Sensor data collection and interpretation
- Sensor fusion
- Virtual world model updating
- AI action planning
- Car controls command issuance

Another key aspect of AI self-driving cars is that they will be driving on our roadways in the midst of human driven cars too. There are some pundits of AI self-driving cars that continually refer to a utopian world in which there are only AI self-driving cars on the public roads. Currently there are about 250+ million conventional cars in the United States alone, and those cars are not going to magically disappear or become true Level 5 AI self-driving cars overnight.

Indeed, the use of human driven cars will last for many years, likely many decades, and the advent of AI self-driving cars will occur while there are still human driven cars on the roads. This is a crucial point since this means that the AI of self-driving cars needs to be able to contend with not just other AI self-driving cars, but also contend with human driven cars. It is easy to envision a simplistic and rather unrealistic world in which all AI self-driving cars are politely interacting with each other and being civil about roadway interactions. That's not what is going to be happening for the foreseeable future. AI self-driving cars and human driven cars will need to be able to cope with each other. Period.

Returning to the topic of YIMBY versus NIMBY and AI self-driving cars, I'd like to take a look at the present and likely future state of this matter.

First, right now, there is much more of a YIMBY that a NIMBY when it comes to AI self-driving cars. There is an exciting allure about AI self-driving cars. It is exhilarating and offers great promise. There is a kind of prestige associated with this new technology. Most things associated with AI are hot right now, and this applies to self-driving cars too.

A community might be eager to tryout these new-fangled futuristic AI self-driving cars. We've seen plenty of sci-fi movies about how the world will eventually have self-driving cars, and why not be one of the first communities to have them. Your community might become known globally for being the first, or at least one of the first, as a showcase for the advent of AI self-driving cars. Imagine if your community had been the birthplace of the Kitty Hawk and the origins of man-made flight.

In one sense, it is a somewhat easy decision to make in terms of YIMBY, because the investment by the community is minimal and the ability to change their viewpoint is highly flexible and can quickly be changed.

Unlike putting in a factory that might require a fixed asset and lots of local monies, the agreement to allow AI self-driving cars can be done nearly without spending a dime by the community. No special facilities are needed, no costly investments to be made locally. The auto maker or tech firm might need to establish a base in the community to house the AI self-driving cars, along with the AI developers and those maintaining the self-driving cars. This is a relatively small investment and offers some advantages to the community such as jobs and taxes to be paid, but overall it is not likely going to be much of either one. The odds are that the auto maker or tech firm will bring into the community the needed skilled specialists and not much local hiring is likely.

Having the AI self-driving cars in the community might be an attractor for other purposes. Perhaps the community can become more well-known, if it today is more of a sleeper kind of locale that not many know about. Or, maybe it is known for say tourism but not for industry. The advent of AI self-driving cars in that locale might create a perception to others that the locale is well-suited for industry. It now has the hottest technology in terms of AI and self-driving cars. It might be seen by other tech firms as a place to also locate their businesses, regardless of whether being into AI self-driving cars or not.

There's a prestige factor that can have a multiplier effect on a community. Having AI self-driving cars might spur the community in other indirect ways. Perhaps the educational system becomes inspired and it rallies teachers, administrators, and students to be interested in tech and STEM (Science, Technology, Engineering and Mathematics). Businesses might opt to invest in tech, having nothing to do with AI self-driving cars per se and more akin to becoming avid tech embracers.

Local leaders might be elated to have AI self-driving cars in their community as it shows a measure of positive outlook and progressiveness. No luddites here, they might say. This could attract other investments into the community by businesses that see the local leadership as supportive of new innovations. An influx of new residents might arise as they perceive the locale to be betting on the future rather than mired in the past.

There is also the potential benefits from a new form of ridesharing. Communities that are first to adopt AI self-driving cars might enjoy the presumed benefits of the increased mobility that AI self-driving cars promises. Pundits believe that we are heading towards a mobility as an economy kind of society, which perhaps these initially adopting communities will experience sooner than other communities.

We've so far discussed the basis for the YIMBY perspective for a local community that opts to either invite in AI self-driving cars or that is approached about allowing for AI self-driving cars in that locale.

What about the NIMBY perspective?

Some might assert that the existing driving regulations don't allow for AI self-driving cars and stand pat that the law is the law. For communities that are willing to change their driving laws to allow for AI self-driving cars, which might also involve aspects of the state driving laws and federal regulations, this could be somewhat of a cost to undertake.

The cost would also possibly involve "political" capital in that the push to put in place laws that are more conducive to AI self-driving cars might be seen by some as wrong or ill-conceived, and later harm or cause the ouster of local leaders by voting against them or otherwise not welcoming their ongoing tenure.

There is also the specter of class action lawsuits against AI self-driving cars and the auto makers and tech firms, for which this might dampen enthusiasm for AI self-driving cars depending upon the outcomes, and if so it could undermine those local leaders that had earlier been a proponent of self-driving cars.

There is a risk to the community that an AI self-driving car might cause or be involved in a car crash, or perhaps strikes a pedestrian, or runs over a dog, or in some manner gets entangled in a matter that cause injury or harm or causes property damage such a running into a wall or a light post. There is ongoing debate about the nature and severity of this kind of risk.

One of the most notable examples was the Uber self-driving car incident that occurred in Phoenix, which I've extensively discussed and analyzed. The matter involved a self-driving car that ran into a pedestrian that was walking a bike across the street, doing so at nighttime and not in a marked crosswalk. Uber opted to temporarily suspend their trials and performed an internally sponsored review, and meanwhile external entities are undertaking their reviews.

Building trust and faith about AI self-driving cars is a matter that takes a lot of time and attention to undertake. It is like filling up a pool or tub and the water takes quite a while to pour into it. Meanwhile, losing trust and faith can happen very quickly, almost like pulling out the plug and the water suddenly drains out.

I've predicted that early adopting communities will be quick to change their minds about AI self-driving car adoption if the instances of injury, death, or damages should arise.

This change of heart and mind can occur in an instant, particularly if the incident is severe enough. Mitigating factors about why or how the incident occurred might help to soften the blow to the YIMBY, but it will certainly take off the glow and likely cast suspicion, plus a tight leash will be the potential consequence such that if another such matter arises, even if one less severe, it could cause the YIMBY to flip over to a NIMBY.

There is also the aspect of portraying AI systems, such as AI self-driving cars, as a danger overall to society. Some might liken an AI self-driving car to a kind of Frankenstein, suggesting it is a monster that needs to be caged or curtailed. Some are worried that once we've opened the door to AI self-driving cars, it will become a widespread takeover of our freedom and liberty, and who knows where the rampant AI will stop, if ever. These conspiracy theorists are on the look for the smallest signs of such a potential.

There are those that believe AI is headed towards a singularity. Perhaps AI will develop and become a sentiment being, of which, the assumption by some is that it will squash humans like a bug. There is also the infamous paperclip AI dilemma, namely that a so-called super-intelligent AI system might try to maximize an aspect such as making paperclips, doing so at the cost of destroying inadvertently the rest of mankind in the unbridled quest to make paperclips.

Another possibility for the NIMBY is the potential for the loss of jobs.

This might seem counter-intuitive since the advent of ready mobility by AI self-driving cars is considered by some to be a sure sign of boosting a local economy and providing more jobs. The other side of the coin is that transportation jobs are potentially going to dry up, at least in terms of the driving of vehicles. Presumably, no more human driven ridesharing and so the Uber and Lyft of today that provide income for human drivers will no longer be doing so (it will be AI systems instead driving the ridesharing self-driving cars).

This lack of the need for human drivers could extend to buses, trucks, and other forms of transportation. All of those human drivers could be out of work. The counter-argument is that there might be other newer jobs that arise to replace those human driver jobs, especially if the volume of transport rises. In other words, there might be so much more transportation taking place that it might open avenues for other kinds of jobs.

How does the NIMBY or YIMBY of AI self-driving cars compare to other kinds of backyard disputes?

The adoption of AI self-driving cars into a community is unlike the placement of a nuclear power plant, since the nuclear power plant is a relatively permanent kind of measure and has other massive consequences if something goes severely haywire. In theory, a community that discovers the advent of AI self-driving cars to be a danger to their community can readily stop or boot-out the AI self-driving car adoption, doing so at relatively small cost and effort (though there could be follow-up lawsuits asserting that the community made an unwise choice to begin with and is partially or fully to blame for the incident).

There are some communities that have embraced a closed track or proving grounds approach that can be used for the development and testing of AI self-driving cars. This is a quite different kind of decision about AI self-driving cars in comparison to allowing AI self-driving cars to roam the public roadways in a community. A proving ground involves the setting aside of a relatively permanent piece of land and having fixed improvements built onto that land. In a manner of speaking, this might be more akin to the HQ2 example, though obviously on a much smaller scale. The risk factor is low in terms of danger to the community since the testing of the AI self-driving cars would presumably be primarily tethered to the set aside closed track.

AI self-driving cars as a roaming element in community is more akin to a transitory backyard admittance. It would seem unlikely to have the same kinds of sustaining benefits that say an HQ2 might provide, and nor the large-scale dangers of a nuclear power plant. For AI self-driving cars, the benefits are relatively low for the community in that kind of comparison, while at the same time, the investment by the community is also quite low. Overall, it is somewhat easy to start and somewhat easy to stop the advent of roaming AI self-driving cars in a community.

The risks to the community obviously involve the potential for serious harm if an AI self-driving car does something untoward, though presumably confined to one incident (after which, the community would likely halt or unwind the arrangement). Are the members of the community willing to accept that kind of risk? It is hard for them to likely know what the risk level is.

For example, the AI self-driving cars might be used in a confined geospace. In that case, the risk of a haywire AI self-driving car is presumably only going to occur in that geographical area of the community, if something untoward does occur. There is the use of back-up human drivers to try and reduce the risks of the AI self-driving car getting involved in an incident, though this does not eliminate the risks and I've spoken and written extensively about the false assumptions about the use of back-up human drivers as a fail-safe (nor too will using remote operators provide any heightened reduction of such risk).

Conclusion

For a community considering allowing AI self-driving cars to roam their streets, it is quite a toss-up right now as to whether to be on the YIMBY or the NIMBY camp.

We are still in the early days of AI self-driving car adoption. Their use on public streets is generally being relatively constrained by the auto makers and tech firms. This likely though will begin to widen and expand as the developers become more confident about the safety of their AI self-driving cars. Doing so will likely increase the chances of something untoward happening.

One bad apple in the barrel can spoil the entire barrel. This suggests that if an AI self-driving car does serious injury or death, it could be that the public becomes distrustful of all AI self-driving cars, regardless of whom the auto maker or tech firm might be. It could be a broad stroke casting of aspersions across all AI self-driving cars.

An admonishment voiced by some pundits in the AI self-driving car camp is that society has to be willing to weigh the potential for injury or harm via AI self-driving cars against the daily injury and harm from human drivers.

This is a rationalist's position that you should be willing to accept some amount of injury or death via AI self-driving cars if it will in-the-end reduce the number of injuries and deaths being caused by human driven cars. Though this might be the case, using such logic is rather hard to stomach from an emotional perspective. People accept the notion that human drivers cause injury and harm, and this is bad, and something should be done about it, but offering a solution that will produce injury or harm, even if less so than human drivers, involves a kind of strict adherence to numbers logic that is nearly unimaginable by most.

The media is a factor in this matter too.

For now, the media has been relatively supportive of the advent of AI self-driving cars, typically offering gee-whiz kinds of coverage. That being said, the media loves too the man-bites-dog story. The media will readily turn against AI self-driving cars if an incident occurs that gets the media riled up. Nothing more the media tends to relish than a love them or hate them kind of situation, which will surely attract eyeballs. Don't be surprised if the media swings overnight from AI self-driving cars as the do-all and best thing since sliced bread to becoming the worst malady to ever be made by mankind.

NIMBY or YIMBY.

YIMBY or NIMBY.

Probably the most predictable aspect is that we'll see communities vacillating from one posture or another when it comes to the initial tryout of AI self-driving cars, and only time will tell which backyard, if any, will be putting out a "Welcome Here" sign or putting up a "Warning: Stay Out" sign instead.

CHAPTER 4

TOP TRENDS OF 2019
AND
AI SELF-DRIVING CARS

CHAPTER 4

TOP TRENDS OF 2019

AND AI SELF-DRIVING CARS

Editor's Note: *This is a end-of-year 2018 compilation of predictions for 2019 about the anticipated emerging trends in AI and self-driving cars. If you are reading this and it is past 2019, you might find these predictions interesting as a viewpoint of what had been earlier forecasted.*

The end of 2018 is in sight. Besides making resolutions for next year, it is timely to make predictions too. How will AI advance next year? What will happen in the realm of AI self-driving cars during 2019? Will it be a good year or a bad year for the advent of this high-tech moonshot that will utterly transform our society?

Achieving true AI self-driving cars will be a crucial evidentiary application of AI for two major reasons.

First, if AI can be developed and deployed for a real-world complex human-based task such as driving a car, it would mean that the field of AI has made tremendous strides and likely a large number of other kinds of hard problems can also be handled via AI. Thus, the driving of a car is merely an exemplar that has forced AI to move forward sufficiently to take on an extremely challenging task that heretofore only cognitively aware humans could do.

Second, the aspect that we would no longer presumably need humans to drive a car and that the driving of a car could entirely be done by an AI system means that the nature of driving and the mobility

71

by society will be radically altered. , I've expressed support many times for the rather bold assertions that true AI self-driving cars will shape a future consisting of mobility-as-a-service and that our economy will become an economic engine fueled and shaped around mobility.

The rub is whether we'll get there without a great deal of torment and hand-wringing, and the other key factor involves the timing of when this will all come to fruition. Timing prophecies are emblazoned with both reasoned and wild speculation.

For those of you that are familiar with my stance on the substance of AI self-driving cars, I am generally upbeat about the potential for AI self-driving cars to reach true autonomous capabilities, but I am also one of the first to detect and persistently point out the hyperbole that often seems to catch-hold about this emerging innovation. Perhaps I grew-up becoming disappointed that I am not today using a jetpack to get around for work and play. Based on this "traumatic disillusionment" of my childhood, I try to bring a realistic and deeply probing perspective about AI, digging as far under-the-hood as necessary to explain what AI can and cannot really do.

As a former professor and AI Lab researcher and director, I relish jumping into the AI minutiae and details to see what really is making the clock tick, so to speak. I'm not a fan of those that wave their hands and tell us to look the other way and just believe in the magic of AI. No magic, please. We need to know what the innards of any AI system consists of, else we can falsely believe that something is possible that really is not. Truth in AI. That's one of my enduring and endearing goals for providing you with my ongoing probing analyses.

Here's then my carefully assembled Top 10 list of predictions about AI self-driving cars for 2019. It is going to be an exciting year, involving some moments of triumph that will seem heartening, which will then be blunted by the sad and fully anticipated AI self-driving car untoward incidents that are going to happen. Mark my words, we are not going to escape injury and death during 2019 by the "hands" of AI self-driving cars. It will happen.

My hope is that those moments of shock and outrage arising by such incidents will spark greater attention to the safety aspects of AI self-driving cars. There also needs to be increased public understanding about the realities of using our public roadways as part of this grand experiment seeking to achieve AI self-driving cars. It will take a village, so to speak, for all to come together toward arriving at true AI self-driving cars. This is not a journey being solely undertaken by AI developers as employed by the automotive and high-tech community. All hands-on-deck, including the general public, regulators, the media, and other stakeholders, if we are going to get through this arduous process successfully.

My ongoing coverage of AI will continue and I've listed below some of the topics I've already got planned to cover in 2019 (see item #10 on my list below). As per my usual style for these matters, I like to address topics that are broadly applicable to AI in any realm, allowing anyone interested in the AI field to become more informed broadly about the latest AI technologies and techniques, and then I demonstrate how the chosen AI topic meshes into the real-world by showcasing its particular application to AI self-driving cars.

In that sense, my column is about the topic of AI and it just so happens to indicate how AI is applied to AI self-driving cars. On the other hand, one might say that my column is about AI self-driving cars and how the realm of self-driving cars is both using and driving forward (pun!) to push AI. What's that, how can my column be on two topics at the same? Easy answer. It is about both. I cover what's up with AI. I also cover what's up with AI self-driving cars.

Any insightful discussion about AI should (in my opinion) offer an indication about what use it can be applied to, which, in my case, I tend to use self-driving cars as that keystone. In a similar manner, any discussion about AI self-driving cars should explain how AI fits in and what the AI can and cannot do.

Duality. That's my coverage. Tackle the tough aspects of AI. Explain, explore, and predict where AI is heading. And, tackle the emergence of AI self-driving cars. Explain, explore and predict where AI self-driving cars are heading. Push further forward on AI. Push further forward on self-driving cars. That's something to look forward to for 2019.

I'll be including herein as handy references for you some of the especially notable pieces that I've already covered on these matters (per feedback by my readers). Perhaps over the holidays you might be interested in catching up with my tales of success and woe in the state-of-the-art AI. Enjoy!

Predictions for 2019

Trumpets blare. The secret scroll is unraveled, and Latin words are spoken. It is time for the 2019 prophecies to be cast upon the world.

Well, that being said, here's indeed my list of 2019 predictions, which is numbered merely for ease of reference and not due to any particular prioritization. Each of the predictions has its own distinct merits and I wouldn't want the sequence of the list to suggest any particular prediction is more so or less so important than the other. In addition, the set of them should be construed in a collective context, rather than interpreting them as separate and distinct notions. In other words, they interact and combine with each other.

My top 10 AI Trends Insider predictions about AI and AI self-driving cars for 2019 are:

1. AI Deep Learning Gets Deeper, But No Eureka Breakthroughs in 2019

2. Expanded Limited Tryouts of AI Self-Driving Cars Valiantly Pushes On For 2019

3. AI Self-Driving Car Incidents in 2019 Will Be Horridly Inevitable

4. Media Frenzy In 2019 About AI Self-Driving Cars Wildly Vacillates Hot-and-Cold

5. Adverse Incidents of AI Self-Driving Cars In 2019 Gets Safety Finally To The Forefront

6. AI Sensory Devices Emerging In 2019 Invoke Three Words: Smaller, Better, Cheaper

7. Coopetition of AI Firms and Auto Makers Widens and Deepens in 2019

8. Federal Regulations on AI Self-Driving Cars Go To Backburner Until 2020 Elections

9. Bullish 2019 Startups in AI Stoke Market And Many Are In Self-Driving Cars Wheelhouse

10. AI Innovations Charge Ahead In 2019 And The AI Game-Of-Thrones Rebirth Continues

Next, I provide the underlying details for each prediction:

Prediction 1

AI Deep Learning Gets Deeper,
But No Eureka Breakthroughs in 2019

In 2019, we'll have more Deep Learning (DL).

Deep Learning is considered a form of Machine Learning (ML) and referred to as "deep" because it typically makes use of Artificial Neural Networks (ANNs) that exceed the shallower sizing of the ANN's of prior years, doing so by adding many more layers of artificial neurons and adding many more artificial neurons. Furthermore, this is more feasible to do then it once was because of the advent of hardware related exploits to handle this larger size, including specialized processors and also supercomputing. The cost too of that hardware has come down and made it more readily economical to do the DL training and deployment.

I don't though see any breathtaking Eureka-style breakthroughs in DL and ML during 2019.

Please do not be discouraged by that assertion. I want to emphasize that I do see that we'll have even deeper DL and ML, which will likely allow for the tackling of ever more interesting problems for which DL/ML can be a solution. I'm confident that the costs to have DL and ML will continue to drop, which is good, and so it will encourage greater uses and become more widespread.

There will be some interesting tweaks to DL and ML during 2019 and there are going to be novelty uses. Will there be a whopper of a new approach to DL and ML that arises in 2019? No. The year 2019 will be more of a grind it out, do more with what we've gotten underway, and see what can happen when the size of DL and ML continues to increase and increase and the costs to do so decrease and decrease.

Prediction 2

Expanded Limited Tryouts of AI Self-Driving Cars Valiantly Pushes On For 2019

The auto makers and tech firms are going to continue onward with their limited tryouts of AI self-driving cars on our public roadways in 2019.

These limited tryouts are intended to see if AI self-driving cars can handle the real-world driving tasks as encountered in, well, the real-world. There is only so much that can be done on a closed track or in a proving ground. There is only so much that can be done via simulations. It is believed that the only way to really get AI self-driving cars ready for driving on public roadways is to put them onto public roadways.

Of course, this is kind of a Catch-22. Some say that we should "perfect" AI self-driving cars before putting them onto the public roadways, but the counter-argument is that we'll never reach that point without actually allowing AI self-driving cars onto public roadways. Yet, if we allow "unproven" AI self-driving cars onto our public roadways and the results are untoward, it could cause the babe to get tossed out with the bath water, namely it could cause the public to reject entirely the AI self-driving car efforts.

It is a bit of a conundrum. Allow AI self-driving cars to drive on our public roads? Yes, because it will provide the kind of experiences needed to successfully drive on the public roads. No, because it endangers the public and could not only cause harm, it could curtail the effort by starting an unstoppable public backlash.

For 2019, the interest in AI self-driving cars is keen enough, along with the ongoing glory and prestige that comes with combining AI with cars, and the salivating billions or trillions of dollars that ultimately can be earned via AI self-driving cars, that the auto makers and tech firms will expand their public tryouts.

I'd wager a bet that this will be done in a somewhat more timid manner than had previously been the case, partially due to the Uber incident in Phoenix in 2018 that led to the death of a pedestrian (along with various other self-driving car related incidents that occurred).

These incidents are a helpful wake-up call for many in the AI and high-tech field that had the classic Silicon Valley "fail first, fail fast" mindset – which might be suitable in some circumstances, but in the case of AI self-driving cars that can cause life-or-death results, perhaps the "fail" part should be given a bit more attention and weight than normal.

AI Self-Driving Car Incidents in 2019
Will Be Horridly Inevitable

I do not want to be the bearer of bad news. Nor do I want anyone in 2019 to get into harm's way. Unfortunately, inevitably, there are going to be adverse incidents involving AI self-driving cars on our public roadways in 2019. It is going to happen. Brace yourself.

There will be incidents involving Level 2 self-driving cars, for which a human driver is supposed to be present and attentive and ready to undertake the driving task. I've frequently written and spoken about the dangers that the co-sharing of the driving task entails. Humans are likely to become complacent, they are likely to become distracted, they are likely to misunderstand their co-sharing role, and so on. There is a litany of ways in which the man-machine aspects of co-sharing a real-time task can readily go awry.

As Level 3 self-driving cars come into the market, I've already predicted this will actually further exacerbate the problem, rather than somehow ameliorating it. This is due to the aspect that the better the AI systems seem to get, the more the human driver will tend toward obviating their duty to aid in driving the car. It is a deathly spiral and we'll have to see how this plays out (perhaps less badly than I think, or so I hope).

Rather than contending with the AI and human driver co-sharing potential debacle, there are some auto makers and tech firms that are trying to jump instead to the Level 4 and Level 5 of self-driving cars. This involves either radically reducing the human driver requirement or eliminating the need for a human driver entirely.

Why not then abandon the Level 2 and Level 3 altogether, you might be wondering.

Because the jury is still out as to whether or not we can really get to the vaunted Level 4 and Level 5, and if so, when we will get there. Meanwhile, it is tempting and possible to continue to add AI and AI-like features to cars that makes them Level 2 and Level 3 ready, and the market hunger is presumably there that is waiting expectantly to get those features.

The plentiful hunger needs to be fed, commensurate with the kind of money to be made, and perhaps brand loyalty to be had too. This feeding though carries great risks and the cooks might discover they offered up the wrong meal.

Prediction 4

Media Frenzy In 2019 About AI Self-Driving Cars Wildly Vacillates Hot-and-Cold

The media, all powerful, the makers and breakers of those both big and small.

There are many in the media that have no idea what an AI self-driving car is, nor the levels of AI self-driving cars, and otherwise consider all so-called "self-driving cars" to be the same. They sometimes call them "robot" cars, which I find misleading because it tends to invoke images of a human-like walking and talking robot that is going to be driving our cars.

Anyway, there is an abundance of what I call "fake news" about AI self-driving cars. It can be due to the reporters that do not know what they are reporting on. It can be due to the reporters having the wool pulled over their eyes, for which they don't realize that it is taking place. It can sometimes be a herd mentality, involving one reporter that states something and other reporters rush to report the same thing, doing so without taking the time and interest to ferret out the merits of the matter.

To-date, I'd say that the mass media has been relatively favorable toward AI self-driving cars. When something untoward happens, there is a momentary questioning about the advent of AI self-driving cars, but it pretty much loses attention as the ravenous media cycle of new news overtakes the story. The rest of the time the coverage is usually the gee-whiz kind of breathless indication of a glorious future as a result of AI self-driving cars.

During 2019, I believe that the media is going to find itself getting hotter and colder about AI self-driving cars.

The intensity of excitement about AI self-driving cars will heighten at times, partially due to the incremental tryouts of AI self-driving cars, providing more widespread interest and media reporting. At the same time, since

81

I am also anticipating that we'll have more adverse incidents, the media is going to whipsaw over to the opposition of these public roadway tryouts.

It is going to be a love 'em and hate 'em kind of year for AI self-driving cars by the vacillating mass media.

Adverse Incidents of AI Self-Driving Cars
In 2019 Gets Safety Finally To The Forefront

Safety has not been as much at the forefront of AI self-driving cars as you might assume. Indeed, I would say that safety in AI overall is a topic that has not been given due attention. The rush towards developing and fielding AI system will ultimately be brushed back when the safety elements become more pronounced.

Similar to how the privacy aspects of data collection and use by the major social media companies was an "unknown" that seemed to suddenly burst onto the scene in 2018 (though insiders knew this was a ticking timebomb), so too will the safety aspects of various kinds of AI systems begin to more overtly rear its head (another ticking timebomb).

I was pleased and honored to participate in a crucial and pioneering AI self-driving car safety summit in 2018 that was sponsored by Velodyne, a major LIDAR vendor. It was encouraging that the AI self-driving car stakeholders are coming together to get on top of the safety issue before it is slammed down upon the industry, which mark my words, it will be.

With my other Top 10 predictions of more AI self-driving car incidents taking place in 2019, and with the media attention and whipsawing, you can be assured that 2019 will force de majeur awareness of safety and AI self-driving cars. Indeed, already some of the auto makers and tech firms making AI self-driving cars have been hiring "Chief Safety Officers" to aid in their efforts, which is one of those it's-about-time and thank goodness for the realization moment in this industry.

Prediction 6

AI Sensory Devices Emerging In 2019
Invoke Three Words: Smaller, Better, Cheaper

Most people tend to think only about the sensory devices on AI self-driving cars and often tend to neglect the innards that have to do with the actual driving task. The sensors get all the grandeur. This makes sense since we can all readily see and touch a sensory device, whether it is a camera, a LIDAR device (the cones you often see on top of an AI self-driving car), a radar device, an ultrasonic device, and so on.

Those sensory devices steal the show and on the one hand it is justified since without being able to sense the world outside of the AI self-driving car, there is not much else that could take place. The AI system needs to know where other cars are. Where are the pedestrians? Where is the road? These all require the use of sensory devices.

If the sensory devices are not fast enough, or if they are unable to collect data, or if they are flaky and provide excessive noise in their data collection, it severely undermines the efforts of the AI self-driving car.

Fortunately, there is a lot of push going on about improving the sensory devices. In three words, smaller, better, cheaper is the mantra for 2019. Expect to see advances in the sensor devices. Expect to see improvements in the software that makes use of those sensors.

<u>Prediction 7</u>

Coopetition of AI Firms and Auto Makers
Widens and Deepens in 2019

AI firms want into the self-driving car realm. It's a fascinating use of AI and one that provides the scale factor that gets the adrenalin pumping. There's money to be made in them thar hills too. Plus, heaven forbid that the auto makers themselves somehow try to usurp the grand AI powers of the high-tech firms and make a go into the AI arena on their own. How dare they!

Auto makers realize that have to be in the self-driving car realm or else lose their shirts. Auto firm stock prices are both emboldened by announcements about AI self-driving cars and at times are pounded down by such announcements. The marketplace and stock market look at this as a horse race and whichever horse seems to be leading at the moment, it helps that horse and pummels the others (unless the others appear to be gaining on that horse).

You've also got the ridesharing firms enmeshed into this mix too. They cannot allow themselves to be left on the side of the road. Auto makers might use the advent of AI self-driving cars to become new defacto ridesharing firms, wiping out the existing lot that had a brief moment in the sun. High tech firms might do the same and wipe out the ridesharing firms.

Often eyeing each other warily, the high-tech firms and the auto makers and the ridesharing firms are all on the same merry-go-round right now. Who will last? Who will get thrown off? Is it better to go it alone or try to join forces in some fashion? Top executives are losing sleep over this, I assure. Go ahead, ask them what keeps them up at night and the answer is going to be AI self-driving cars.

I've already predicted and indeed it has been shown that there is a lot of coopetition occurring in this industry. Coopetition is a blending of cooperation and competition.

During 2019, we'll see more of it. Companies that you never thought might partner will do so. Companies that partnered will at times enjoy the leverage, and some will come to regret it. Not all partnerships are meant to last. Time will tell.

<u>Prediction 8</u>

Federal Regulations on AI Self-Driving Cars
Go To Backburner Until 2020 Elections

Regulators are not quite sure what to do about AI self-driving cars. They don't want to be overly regulatory, which can get the backlash that they are hampering innovation. High-tech is still the high horse and the public seems to relish the grand new inventions that are being churned out. Imagine if you were an elected official that got labeled as slowing down the advent of AI self-driving cars or maybe stopped it altogether.

This is a tough spot to be in as a regulator. Besides the Luddite charges of impinging on modern-day progress, there is also the hoped-for claim that AI self-driving cars will eliminate or at least reduce the number of lives lost due to car incidents. What regulator can withstand the brunt of not willing to save human lives!

On the other hand, if AI self-driving cars while on our public roadways in 2019 cause damage, injury, or death, you can bet that the public is going to go after regulators that are after-the-fact perceived as being overly lenient. The potential torrent of anger will likely get those regulators booted out, even if they had little to do with the matter or otherwise might suggest that they were relying on the advice of experts. There will likely be a price to be paid, no matter what a regulator might offer as a defense.

There have been ongoing efforts in Congress to try and pass new laws related to AI self-driving cars. This effort has gone back-and-forth and at this writing is still in regulatory limbo. Will it pass in 2019? The odds would seem low. The year of 2019 is the lead-in to the 2020 elections. Does the passage of an AI self-driving car bill warrant the regulators attention in 2019?

If they pass a law that helps promote AI self-driving cars, it might be handy and they could try to use this as a supportive point when running in 2020 for the elections. But, if AI self-driving cars have had recurring incidents in 2019, and the media has turned negative about

AI self-driving cars, and if the law so passed was a contributor towards allowing such incidents (or, at least didn't try to curtail it), those regulators will get tarnished coming into 2020.

The organic approach will more likely be that the AI self-driving car law will continue to bump along and be debated. Unless there is a pressing need to get it passed, it will languish until after the 2020 elections.

The pressing need to get it passed would primarily be if there were recurring incidents involving AI self-driving cars, and in that case the regulators could try to rapidly toughen the law and get it on the books. This might then be a handy tool for the 2020 election campaigns.

<u>Prediction 9</u>

Bullish 2019 Startups in AI Stoke Market
And Many Are In Self-Driving Cars Wheelhouse

I'm bullish about 2019 for AI related startups. I work with a number of high-tech startups as a mentor, and participate too with several startup incubators and accelerators, plus I am a serial entrepreneur in my own right (meaning that I've launched, run, and sold several high-tech firms). I also serve as a pitch competition judge, mainly in Silicon Valley and Silicon Beach.

There are a bunch of start-ups that are right now in the concepts stage that will emerge during 2019. Venture capital (VC) and Private Equity (PE) are still eager to find and fund those high-tech start-ups that appear to have something that might be able to hit the ball out of the park.

In one of my 2018 articles, I discussed the nature of AI startups in the AI self-driving car niche. This will continue in 2019 as a hot area to have a startup. Thanks goes to those readers that sent me info about their proposed startups, of which some I've now gotten underway aiding them with their formulation.

Predictions 10

AI Innovations Charge Ahead In 2019
And The AI Game-Of-Thrones Rebirth Continues

Here's some key upcoming aspects for 2019 that will emerge as important elements:

- Deep Personalization in AI

- Emergency-Only AI

- Game Theory and AI

- Byzantine Generals Problem and AI

- Brute Force Algorithms and AI

- Chess Playing and AI

- Empathetic Computing

- Perpetual Computing

- Big Data and AI: The Case of AI Self-Driving Cars

- Cobots and AI Self-Driving Cars

- Crumbling Roadway Infrastructure and Self-Driving Cars

- Anomaly Detection Advances for AI

- Multi-Party Privacy and AI

- Hyperlanes versus Bullet Trains and AI Self-Driving Cars

- Sports Cars and AI Self-Driving Cars

- System Load Balancing in AI

- Rewilding of AI Self-Driving Cars

- Bug Bounty in AI

AI will continue as gangbusters during 2019. We'll see more adoption of AI systems. We'll see more advances in AI technologies and techniques. There will be a hint of concern about AI biases, and a large dose of AI safety qualms, for which I am hoping that the AI community can step-up to the plate and appropriately tackle.

CHAPTER 5

RURAL AREAS
AND
AI SELF-DRIVING CARS

CHAPTER 5

RURAL AREAS
AND AI SELF-DRIVING CARS

The countryside can be a breathtaking relief from the confines of the big city and the suburbs. In the United States, any geographical area that is not considered within an urban area is generally considered the countryside, often referred to simply as a rural area. Typically, a rural area in the United States is sparsely populated. The population density is relatively low and the landscape is rather large. You can often drive across a rural area for miles upon miles and see nothing other than rolling hills, majestic mountains, open flat lands, and often times large-scale farms.

Whenever I drive from the bustling and freeway-clogged environ of Los Angeles up to the Silicon Valley area in Northern California, it is a splendor to witness the Central California portion of the state. The inland and non-coastal route consists of around 450 miles that provides more than half of the vegetables, nuts, and fruits that are grown in the United States.

Many tourists are surprised to discover that California has an agricultural belt all of its own. If you come to do touristy kinds of activities, you'd likely go to see Hollywood and Disneyland in Southern

California, and perhaps go up to San Francisco to see the Golden Gate Bridge and ride the famous trollies, but otherwise would not consider spending much time in the central rural area unless you had keen interest in farms and ranches.

Next time that you find yourself munching on almonds, apricots, tomatoes, grapes, asparagus, and other such delicious items, please make sure to thank California since the odds are high that those items were grown in our central inland areas. Driving on the main route from Los Angeles to San Francisco, consisting of either highway 5 or the CA 99, you can pretty much expect to see farms that appear to stretch to the horizon. When it is growing season, there are zillions of rows of crops being grown. When the crops have been harvested, it becomes an endless dirt patch that awaits being planted for the next iteration of the agricultural cycle.

I remember one time that I opted to visit one of the farms while making my way on the Interstate 5. It was going to be an interesting visit since I hadn't been on a working farm for many ages (when my children were young, I often took them to visit a farm, so they could see what goes on in the rural areas and learn how our food is grown). For this visit, I had prearranged to meet with a farmer to discuss some of the advances taking place in AgriTech, which is the term used to refer to the advent of high-tech being infused into agriculture.

Side note, there's ample opportunity to combine AI with AgriTech and doing so is considered a next wave of high-tech for the agricultural realm. For those of you looking for fertile ground to use AI, consider agriculture.

Sheepishly, I admit that I was expecting to see a farmhouse that did not have indoor plumbing, barely had electricity, and the work on the farm was being done by horse and plows. Ouch! I realized that I'd been to too many old-time farms that are more Disneyland-like than the real thing. When I got to the farm on this more recent trip, I was impressed at the high-tech aspects involved in contemporary farming. They had a satellite dish to make sure they could keep tabs on the prices of commodities and were quite sophisticated in their crop management and forecasting. Much of the farming equipment was high-tech equipped and it was apparent that I needed to update my mental model about what happens on a farm.

It was also fascinating to realize that when the families that lived in these rural areas often drove to the nearest town to get supplies or get their children to school, they lamented that it took maybe thirty to forty-five minutes each way to do so. I say this is fascinating because my daily commute for work in traffic frenzied Los Angeles is more than an hour each way, and yet the distance I travel is a fraction of the distance they needed to go.

If they were complaining about a 30-minute to 45-minute drive, it made me shrug and stifle a mild laugh, since I endure an hour or more drive. Plus, I might add forlornly, my hour drive is not nearly as pretty and serene. My freeway driving consists of looking at the backs of cars and seeing garish billboards, rather than admiring stately looking cows in pastures and seeing budding tomatoes on the vine).

In other words, though some might mistake the distance as being a huge factor while driving in a rural area, it could amount to the same amount of driving time as driving while in the suburbs and big cities.

My commute is bogged down by lots of traffic and the speed I can go is maybe an average of 15-20 miles per hour. For rural driving, there is usually much less traffic and the average speed can be more akin to 40 to 60 miles per hour. Ironically, it seems, their driving time and my driving time is about the same, even though the distance covered is quite different.

In Los Angeles, I am confronted with cars that want to play bumper bashing games, along with pedestrians that dart across busy streets and cause the drivers to radically hit their brakes, playing a kind of Frogger game. You probably would at first assume that driving in rural areas would be a grand relief since there would presumably not be the aspects of cars within inches of each other and nutty pedestrians that are willing to risk their lives to get across the street like a chicken with its head cut-off.

Surprisingly, according to stats provided by governmental highway agencies, car related fatalities in rural areas was nearly 50% of the traffic deaths in the United States, and yet the percentage of the U.S. population in rural areas is only around 20%. Thus, driving in the rural areas is actually a lot more dangerous than you might imagine.

There are various theories about why the driving fatalities rate per capita is so high in the rural areas in comparison to the urban and city areas.

Some say that it is due to the curved roads in rural areas, preventing drivers from seeing around a bend, or perhaps taking curves too fast and skidding into an accident. Another guess is that the lack of street lighting at night in many rural areas makes it more likely that drivers will not see objects or the roadway or other cars, and therefore the drivers are more apt to hit something than in an urban area that is replete with street lighting. A somewhat popular theory is that the drivers go very fast in rural areas, being unencumbered by other traffic, and they get themselves into driving troubles that they cannot readily get out of, due to a lack of response time if they had instead been going slower.

There is also the vaunted "highway hypnosis" that can cause a driver to get into a car accident. I remember when learning to drive that my driving instructor warned us about the dangers of highway hypnosis. If you aren't familiar with the phrase itself, I'm sure you are familiar with what it consists of. Mainly, it has to do with become zombie-like as a driver when you are driving over large distances in a monotonous landscape and with little or no traffic.

What seems to happen is that your mind becomes dulled, perhaps doing so due the lack of any changing scenery and the nonuse of your thinking processes to handle the driving task. One might say that you are mentally on autopilot.

I remember one terrifying time that I was driving on a country road and doing so for hours on end, and all of a sudden, a deer darted across the road. This was by far worse than any pedestrian in the city darting across the road because I was completely mentally ill-prepared for the deer. Sure, there were lots of deer crossing warning signs, but when you don't actually see any deer for hours at a time, you mentally begin to disregard the signs. Maybe the signs are only meant to scare you into going slower, you perhaps begin to think, or the deer only cross at a certain time of the year and by luck you aren't driving on the roads at that time of the year (so your mind blanks out the possibility of a deer appearing any time soon).

When the deer leapt onto the road ahead of me, I even thought it was either a mirage or a gag. It could be that all the deer roadway warning signs had planted the idea of a deer into my brain, and so I was imagining that a deer was suddenly in the roadway. Or, I figured it was maybe a fake deer, a mannequin deer, which had fallen off the back of a truck that was on its way to setup a Christmas display showcasing Santa and his reindeer.

All in all, it took me a solid several seconds to register in my mind that it was an actual deer, and it was actually in my way, and I was actually going to hit it. Thankfully, I swerved, and it moved, so we missed hitting each other, though this took maybe a year or two off my lifetime due to the scare and panic that struck me when it happened. I guess you could say that I was in the grip of highway hypnosis that led to my dulled response (that's what I was going to have my attorney allege at trial, if I got busted for hitting a deer, if I had struck it!).

Besides the trance or zombie kind of mental state, there's another kind of mental trickery that can befall you while driving in a rural area. It is called velocitation. This consists of getting used to going at a high speed and causing you to gradually lose awareness of how fast you are really going. You've certainly experienced this. The most likely scenario involves coming off a freeway where you had been going 65 miles per hour and driving onto an off-ramp that is rated at perhaps 30 miles per hour.

When you get onto the on-ramp, you might not realize you are going over twice the speed as recommended for the off-ramp. If you start to brake to ease off the 65 miles per hour, going at say 50 miles per hour might seem like you are going at 30 miles per hour. In essence, going even just slightly slower seems like you are going a lot slower. Your mind gets messed-up about being able to gauge your true speed.

Let's then add to our list of reasons why rural driving is dangerous by including the potential for getting your mind immersed into highway hypnosis, and also that you might become mentally stagnant about your speed and suffer from velocitation. Of course, these same kinds of mental maladies can occur for drivers in urban areas too. I mention this to emphasize that it is not something that only occurs in rural driving. I'd say it is more prone to occur and more likely to happen with greater frequency for rural drivers, which arises because of the prevalent driving landscape involved in rural areas.

Here's another aspect about rural driving that is generally more prevalent in rural areas than in other areas, namely the classic unmarked driveways, entrances, exits, and crossroads. In the normal city driving and suburbia driving, the odds are high that any driveway into or out of a house or property is going to be well-marked and readily seen. Same is the case for entrances into a mall or exits from a school ground. Sure, there might be the occasional exceptions, but I dare say it is usually painted or posted and made apparent by local transportation authorities because of the volume of traffic that goes nearby.

When I drove out to the farm to visit the modern-day farmer, I ended-up on some backroads by mistake. There were roads that did not appear on my GPS mapping system. There were hardly any posted signs. The entrance into some of the roads was hidden by trees and other items. I also nearly got banged into by a pick-up truck that sprung from a driveway that I did not see. The pick-up truck was akin to the deer that I had encountered. Yes, I realize that I should be expecting to see pick-up trucks while driving around farms, but having one just dart out from an unmarked driveway caught me off-guard (we didn't collide, thankfully).

Some call these points at which an unmarked passageway intersects with a fast-moving road to be considered an "instant intersection" and usually is not on a map and is just something that locals know to be watchful about. Locals keep a keen eye for those notorious intersections. An outsider such as me, not being familiar with the roads that I was driving on, could not even predict when those instant intersections were going to "instantaneously" rear their ugly heads. Obviously, if another car wasn't going to come along at those points, it made little difference to me that they existed, and it was only when another vehicle might magically appear that I was then at risk of collision.

Some of you are maybe saying that I was driving too fast. Slow down, Lance! If you don't know where those hidden intersections are, you just need to watch your speed and go slow enough to deal with them when they occur.

I found that trying to go slow in some of these rural locations was perhaps as dangerous as going fast.

When I was going slow, there was bound to be a local that was driving fast (just my luck, I guess). My slowness and when combined with their fastness were often a recipe for disaster. They were barreling down a road that they drive every day and came upon my slow-moving car. At times, besides getting a hefty dose of a horn honking from them, it would tend toward a dangerous moment of my either getting hit by the faster moving car, or the faster moving car went around me and potentially put us both in danger if another car was coming toward us.

I certainly did see the need to watch my speed and knew that there might be slow-moving tractors or other slow-moving vehicles from time-to-time. I've never had a herd of sheep or cows block me while on a rural road, though I did one time have an entire family of ducks. It was one of those memorable driving moments. Up ahead were some ducks, waddling across the street. I slowed down to a crawl and did not want to scare them. I came to a stop some distance from them and watched in amazement as they took their time, waddle, waddle, waddle.

Believe it or not, a friend of mine later told me that I should have driven right up to them and honked my horn. Why, you might ask? He said that by my being quiet, I was deluding them into thinking that going across a car-driven street was safe to do. It would get them into thorny trouble down-the-road, so to speak. If instead I had given them a really big scare, it would have convinced them to never try crossing a street again and presumably someday save their lives. What do you think, did I do a disservice to those cute ducks?

In any case, another factor about rural driving can be the roads at times might not be well maintained. The roads might suffer from heavy vehicles tearing up the asphalt surface. Rains and cold weather can beat-up the road pavement. There can be roads that are merely packed dirt. In foul weather, some roads can become muddy messes, or on a paved road the potholes are hidden by a layer of rain water.

Road signs might not exist or might be torn and worn. I've seen instances of road signs that do exist but are no longer relevant. One said that a gas station was a quarter mile ahead. At the quarter mile mark, there was nothing left but an abandoned set of gas pumps. One sign was a street sign that seemed to mark a street that did not exist and perhaps never did exist, since there wasn't anything that suggested a road had once been where the sign sat. Maybe the sign maker was hopeful that a street would one day be put there, and in a self-fulfilling prophecy kind of way had put up the sign.

In short, rural areas are their own kind of driving realm with a pronounced kind of landscape and driving challenges. You can certainly encounter many of the same kinds of driving challenges in any suburbia or urban area. Rural areas though tend to have more of and a larger-scale kind of specialty driving task aspects.

There's no question that someone that can drive in an urban setting will likely be able to drive in a rural setting, which is important to keep in mind.

I highlight that you can drive in an urban setting and likewise be able to drive in a rural setting because I am trying to indicate that the driving skills are roughly the same.

When I helped my children learn to drive, I didn't particularly have to take them to a rural area so that someday they could drive in a rural area. They learned enough about driving in an urban area that they could readily translate their driving skills into being useful for rural driving.

That being the case, there are subtleties that can make a difference when driving in a rural area. As mentioned, you might need to be wary of highway hypnosis, velocitation, roads that are in bad shape, hidden entrances and driveways, high speeds over lengthy stretches, and deal with other drivers that take their rural roadways for granted and aren't on-the-look for less-familiar with the landscape drivers. There are also the jaywalking ducks and sheep to be dealt with, which I must say are easier on the eyes than those human pedestrians that give you the death-to-all-drivers stare when they are illegally crossing a city street.

What does this have to do with AI self-driving cars?

At the Cybernetic AI Self-Driving Car Institute, we are developing AI software for self-driving cars. One crucial aspect, we believe, involves having the AI be able to drive a self-driving car in rural areas, in addition to being able to drive in the city and urban areas.

Allow me to elaborate.

I'd like to first clarify and introduce the notion that there are varying levels of AI self-driving cars. The topmost level is considered Level 5. A Level 5 self-driving car is one that is being driven by the AI and there is no human driver involved. For the design of Level 5 self-driving cars, the auto makers are even removing the gas pedal, brake pedal, and steering wheel, since those are contraptions used by human drivers. The Level 5 self-driving car is not being driven by a human and nor is there an expectation that a human driver will be present in the self-driving car. It's all on the shoulders of the AI to drive the car.

For self-driving cars less than a Level 5, there must be a human driver present in the car. The human driver is currently considered the responsible party for the acts of the car. The AI and the human driver are co-sharing the driving task. In spite of this co-sharing, the human is supposed to remain fully immersed into the driving task and be ready at all times to perform the driving task. I've repeatedly warned about the dangers of this co-sharing arrangement and predicted it will produce many untoward results.

Let's focus herein on the true Level 5 self-driving car. Much of the comments apply to the less than Level 5 self-driving cars too, but the fully autonomous AI self-driving car will receive the most attention in this discussion.

Here's the usual steps involved in the AI driving task:
- Sensor data collection and interpretation
- Sensor fusion
- Virtual world model updating
- AI action planning
- Car controls command issuance

Another key aspect of AI self-driving cars is that they will be driving on our roadways in the midst of human driven cars too. There are some pundits of AI self-driving cars that continually refer to a utopian world in which there are only AI self-driving cars on the public roads. Currently there are about 250+ million conventional cars in the United States alone, and those cars are not going to magically disappear or become true Level 5 AI self-driving cars overnight.

Indeed, the use of human driven cars will last for many years, likely many decades, and the advent of AI self-driving cars will occur while there are still human driven cars on the roads. This is a crucial point since this means that the AI of self-driving cars needs to be able to contend with not just other AI self-driving cars, but also contend with human driven cars. It is easy to envision a simplistic and rather unrealistic world in which all AI self-driving cars are politely interacting with each other and being civil about roadway interactions. That's not what is going to be happening for the foreseeable future. AI self-driving cars and human driven cars will need to be able to cope with each other.

Returning to the rural area aspects, there are a number of AI driving elements that come to play when an AI self-driving car encounters a rural landscape.

I'd like to first tackle a misconception that seems to be spreading about the notion of AI self-driving cars being deployed in rural areas, namely that it won't be worthwhile to have AI self-driving cars in rural areas.

This notion is exemplified by the December 2018 issue of Automobile magazine, in which there is an article entitled "Autonomous State" by Arthur St. Antoine and an expert on self-driving cars indicates that there is no benefit to having an AI self-driving car in rural areas (see page 95 of the article), asserting that since there is so miniscule of a rural population that it isn't worth having a ride-sharing self-driving car be situated in those parts of the country.

I would certainly argue vehemently that claiming there is no benefit to having an AI self-driving car in a rural area is absolutely wrong.

There are in fact many benefits. If the word "benefit" means that there must be some (one or more) advantages to having an AI self-driving car, doing so over the use of a conventional or legacy car, and if the suggestion is that there is no advantage of having an AI self-driving car over having a conventional car while in rural areas, I believe we can easily poke a hole in that balloon.

When I met with the farmer at his modern-day farmhouse, he indicated that each morning and afternoon he or his wife drove their children to and from the school, taking about 30 to 40 minutes each way to make the drive. This meant that either he or his wife had to leave the farm to simply drive the children to school. It also meant that one of the two (the husband or the wife) was unavailable to work the farm during that driving task.

The farmer also indicated that each day they typically would need to go get supplies from various supply depos that were in various areas of the rural community. Once again, either he or his wife made those drives. And, once again, the driving task denied one of them of actually working the farm since they were only acting as a driver during those supply runs.

I realize you might want to counter-argue that it would be "only" maybe an hour or two of their day to do the driving, but I'd like to point out that this is still nonetheless a drain on their available time to work the farm. Furthermore, here's an added twist that is not simply a labor oriented time-based factor per se.

He mentioned that there have been occasions when their daughter or son was at school and became sick and wanted to come home right away. Usually, unfortunately, he and his wife were both in a remote spot of the farm, each working the land, the cattle, the crops, etc. Upon getting a call from the school, one of them had to quickly get from the remote part of the farm and back to the farmhouse, and then drive from the farmhouse over to the school. This was being done under duress in that they would naturally be concerned about getting to their child as rapidly as they could.

If they had available an AI self-driving car, the self-driving car could routinely take the children back-and-forth to school. This would relieve the farmer and his wife from making the drive and thus add time to their labor efforts towards the farm itself.

The AI self-driving car would also be ready for any emergency situation such as the children getting sick while at school, and could be remotely dispatched by the farmer, electronically commanding it from afar while in the remote areas of the farm. The AI self-driving car would then drive to the school, doing so from the farmhouse, pick-up the child, and whisk the child back to the farmhouse. While inside the AI self-driving car, the camera inside the self-driving car would allow the parents to remotely interact with the child and see how the child was doing.

In short, an AI self-driving car would absolutely aid the farmer and his family, doing so by acting as an automated chauffeur for the children and for making supply runs. I'm sure there are lots of other uses they could come up with for an AI self-driving car.

I also have focused primarily on the rural aspects of a farm, but it should be hopefully self-evident that an AI self-driving car could be handy for other rural landscapes beyond just a farm. With the spread-out nature of a rural area, any kind of human driving is going to likely be time consuming and there are bound to be many kinds of circumstances for which having an AI self-driving car would be highly prized.

Perhaps you live in a rural area and go to work each day, leaving at home your elderly grandma. She is too old to drive a car and cannot get around on her own. With an AI self-driving car, she would have greater mobility. This could come to play on everyday desires of going someplace, and it could also be especially helpful for moments when she might need to see a doctor or go get her medicines.

Okay, I believe I've well-expunged the idea that there is no benefit of an AI self-driving car for rural areas. That was easy. I'll consider that perhaps the notion of "no benefit" was actually meant to be more akin to the idea that there is not a viable ROI (Return on Investment) related to having an AI self-driving car in a rural area.

In other words, you cannot usually look only at benefits when weighing the value of something, but also need to look at the costs too. You then compare the benefits to the costs and try to calculate whether the benefits end-up outweighing the costs. If there is a suitable ROI, you could assert that the benefits are outweighing the costs and therefore the item is worth investing in. If there is not a suitable ROI, you would likely assert that the costs outweigh the benefits and therefore the matter is not likely sensible to invest in.

Therefore, rather than suggesting there aren't any benefits of having an AI self-driving car in a rural area, it would be more sensible for someone to try and argue that there isn't a sufficient ROI. By recasting the argument into the use of an ROI, you can escape the rather obvious counter-pounding that there are indeed clear-cut benefits. The question becomes whether those benefits outweigh the costs or not.

I've previously tackled the topic of ridesharing and AI self-driving cars, and also assessed the affordability of AI self-driving cars for consumers. Allow me to quickly recap some key elements of those relevant topics herein.

Many view that AI self-driving cars will predominantly be used for ride-sharing purposes. This makes sense in that suppose you go to work and need a lift to get there, you might opt to use an AI self-driving car on a ride-sharing basis to do so. It is predicted by some self-driving car pundits that consumers will gradually eschew owning their own car and will mainly use ride-sharing AI self-driving cars as their mode of transportation.

I've broken that kind of thinking about car ownership by pointing out that consumers could presumably do likewise in terms of turning a self-driving car into a ride-sharing money maker for themselves. You use your AI self-driving car to get you to work, and then allow your AI self-driving car the rest of the day to earn money as a ride-sharing service. When you finish your work day, it picks you up and takes you home. While at home at night, you send out your AI self-driving car for further ride-sharing money-making activity.

In that case, your AI self-driving car is a money maker. This allows you to potentially afford the likely higher cost of an AI self-driving car over a conventional car. Owning an AI self-driving car could be a means to make money on-the-side, or it could even become your primary source of making money. Why should the auto makers or ride-sharing firms make that money when you could do so instead? Today, the tough thing is finding human drivers to drive cars, but with the AI self-driving car you have no need to deal with the human driver hiring aspects.

Let's return to the rural setting. I've earlier herein indicated that the population is usually sparsely distributed in a rural locale. The question of making money off an AI self-driving car as a ride-sharing vehicle becomes whether or not the sparseness of the population defeats the potential of making money.

In a big city environ, an AI self-driving car as a ride-sharing vehicle is presumably going to readily have paying riders and do so back-to-back. There will be lots of short rides and many of them in a city or urban setting (hopefully; though this must be tempered by the amount of competition, since it could be that we end-up with zillions of AI self-driving cars all trying to grab the same ride-sharing requests!).

Suppose the farmer that I met had an AI self-driving car. He could use it for taking the kids to school and for doing the other supply depo errands for him. Could he also offer it up as a ride-sharing service to other people in the rural area? Yes, of course. The downside would be that it would likely be spending a lot of its time merely getting to wherever the next customer was and thus not earning money directly per se when it was merely in transit.

In the case of the urban or city setting, many pundits are assuming that an AI self-driving car won't need to use a lot of time to get to its next customer and that customers will be aplenty in a limited geographical distance. I say this because money producing models about AI self-driving cars are often based on the belief that there will be little non-use time and that an AI self-driving car will pretty much continually be totting around paying riders.

I'm not so sure those models are right and are perhaps optimistically assuming that there is little or no competition. The other day, I took a ride-sharing service to the airport and the human driver told me that it was better for him to sit at the airport and wait for his next potential customer, even though there are lots of other ride-sharing vehicles also waiting, versus his getting back into the downtown area to find a customer.

He indicated that the downtown area was a worse random-chance of finding a paying customer and also that the short hops were killing him in that he would get a short hop that paid just a few bucks and then be idle for a long time. He said that by picking up someone from the airport, it would be a longer haul and more money than by simply rushing back into the downtown area.

In the case of rural areas, we cannot axiomatically assume that a ride-sharing use of an AI self-driving car is doomed to a poor or insufficient ROI. It certainly might seem that way and one's intuition seems to suggest it. But, it also depends upon the competition. If every farmer opts to buy an AI self-driving car and do so while living in the same rural area, it would tend to imply that they aren't going to be able to use their AI self-driving car as a money maker since everyone else nearby also has one anyway. On the other hand, if only some buy an AI self-driving car, there is a chance that it could be a money maker in that rural area.

Back to the aspect of whether or not there is any benefit of an AI self-driving car being in a rural area, I'd claim that there is absolutely a benefit. In terms of whether there is a sound ROI, I'd say that we'd need to consider the particulars of a rural area and know more about what the cost of the AI self-driving car will be, along with how much competition there will be. Some rural areas could be handsome ROI's and others not.

I'd like to also re-think this benefits question by turning the question in a different manner. If you take the position that there is no beneficial basis for having an AI self-driving car in a rural area, regardless of how you come to that calculation, you are also then silently asserting that the rural area will continue to use conventional or legacy cars to get around.

Essentially, you are dooming the rural area to continuing with conventional cars or at least AI self-driving cars that are not autonomous.

Pretty quick of you to cast about 20% of the United States population into a bucket wherein they are not able to enjoy the use of AI self-driving cars. Even if those people are widely dispersed, it still seems like a hefty sized market and one that would be foolish to ignore.

Perhaps several farmers might band together to purchase an AI self-driving car and use it as a kind of community-oriented ride-sharing service. Maybe the local community bands together and gets a fleet of AI self-driving cars and uses local tax dollars to run the fleet. My point being that it does not necessarily need to be the case that an AI self-driving car is owned by a single individual or a family.

Another aspect is that we aren't yet calculating in all of this the lost time to doing human driving, in the sense that if the farmer or his wife were able to work the farm longer, what is the value of their time and how does it equate to the cost of the AI self-driving car?

There are also the safety aspects that we probably would be best to consider in all of this discussion about rural areas and AI self-driving cars.

I had mentioned that nearly half of the car fatalities in the United States occur in the rural areas. If that's the case, and if you are suggesting that AI self-driving cars are not "worthwhile" having in rural areas, and if we are to assume that AI self-driving cars will dramatically curtail the death rate of car accidents, you are then condemning the rural areas to continue to be a slaughterhouse based on human driving foibles (that's a bit of hyperbole, which I use only to help make the point herein).

Hopefully, the deploying of AI self-driving cars in rural areas would reduce the chances of getting into a car related fatality. An AI self-driving car needs to be able to avoid getting into any kind of highway hypnosis, which humans fall pray to. An AI self-driving car needs to be able to avoid getting into a velocitation mode, which humans do.

Can an AI self-driving car handle the long stretches of monotonous driving that occurs in rural areas? That certainly ought to be the case.

Can AI self-driving cars cope with the winding curved roads and the unexpected "instant intersections" of poorly labeled driveways and entrances? That's a tougher requirement, for sure. There is an added chance that the AI might do better by the use of Machine Learning (ML) and Deep Learning (DL), wherein the more that any AI self-driving cars cover that same landscape, it could be shared with other AI self-driving cars via cloud-based learning and put them on the same plain as a "local" that is familiar with the roads and their idiosyncratic elements via their use of OTA (Over-The-Air) updating.

Another potential advantage for AI self-driving cars being safer than human drivers could involve the use of V2V (vehicle-to-vehicle) electronic communications, along with V2I (vehicle-to-infrastructure) electronic communications.

I had earlier mentioned that when driving in a rural area, another car came upon me that was moving quite fast and I presumed it was a local that knew well the roads. The other driver was somewhat caught by surprise at my slower moving car. I was somewhat caught by surprise by the other driver that suddenly came upon me.

With AI self-driving cars, the AI of one car could electronically communicate with another AI self-driving car, using V2V, and forewarn the other one that they are both coming upon each other. This could be essential for also dealing with the "instant intersection" situations. Even though one AI self-driving car might not be able to visually or via radar detect another AI self-driving car that is coming out of a driveway that is blocked by a clump of trees, they might be able to communicate via V2V to let each other know of the other one's presence. They would then adjust their driving accordingly.

I've coined the word "omnipresence" to refer to multiple AI self-driving cars that share with each other the status of a roadway. This could be handy for when several AI self-driving cars are in the vicinity of each other and driving on say a mountain road. One AI self-driving car up ahead might alert the others that a deer just darted across the road. Another AI self-driving car might have detected rock debris in the road and alerted the other AI self-driving cars to be wary of the blockage. And so on.

The roadway infrastructure might also communicate with the AI self-driving cars. Via V2I, a hidden driveway might beacon out a message to let any AI self-driving cars driving nearby know that there is a hidden driveway there. Thus, even if there had not yet been any other AI self-driving cars that went past that driveway and could alert others, the beacon itself would do so.

Conclusion

I'd vote that AI developers should be honing AI self-driving cars to be able to drive in rural areas. In spite of some that are suggesting there won't be any benefit of AI self-driving cars being used in rural areas, it is my view that they not only might have a viable ROI numerically, they could also save lives in rural areas, and that would presumably have some economic benefit too.

AI self-driving cars might involve individual ownership by rural livers, and/or it might involve collectives that jointly obtain an AI self-driving car and put it to use in their rural area.

For those AI developers that assume their AI self-driving car will readily work in a rural area if it already works in an urban setting, I'd advise that you reconsider that assumption. There are enough twists and turns to make it worthwhile to enhance the AI to cope specifically with the aspects of rural driving. I had earlier indicated that when I helped my children learn to drive that I had not needed to explicitly cover rural driving, but once they did do some rural driving on their own, they had to learn the nuances thereof. AI developers ought to bake those nuances directly into their AI self-driving car capabilities.

Will an AI self-driving car enjoy watching someone tip over a cow? Probably not. Will an AI self-driving car become captivated by the wide expanse of majestic crops that stretch to the horizon. Better not. Would an AI self-driving car become an essential and valued element in rural living. I'd bet so. We went from horse and plow to conventional cars, and the transformation to AI self-driving cars is likely to be as dramatic and valuable. Rural areas will welcome AI self-driving cars and the benefits will be substantive, you can mark my words on that.

CHAPTER 6

SELF-IMPOSED CONSTRAINTS AND AI SELF-DRIVING CAR

CHAPTER 6

SELF-IMPOSED CONSTRAINTS
AND
AI SELF-DRIVING CAR

Constraints. They are everywhere. Seems like whichever direction you want to move or proceed, there is some constraint either blocking your way or at least impeding your progress. Per Jean-Jacques Rousseau's famous 1762 book entitled "The Social Contract," he proclaimed that mankind is born free and yet everywhere mankind is in chains.

Though it might seem gloomy to have constraints, I'd dare say that we probably all welcome the aspect that arbitrarily deciding to murder someone is pretty much a societal constraint that inhibits such behavior. Movies like "The Purge" perhaps give us insight into what might happen if we removed the criminal constraints or repercussions of murder, which, if you've not seen the movie, let's just say the aspect of providing a 12-hour period to commit any crime that you wish, doing so without any legal ramifications, well, it makes for a rather sordid result. Anarchy, some might say.

There are thusly some constraints that we like and some that we don't like. In the case of our laws, we as a society have gotten together and formed a set of constraints that governs our societal behaviors. One might though contend that some constraints are beyond our ability to overcome, imposed upon us by nature or some other force.

117

Icarus, according to Greek mythology, tried to fly, doing so via the use of wax-made wings, and flew too close to the sun, falling to the sea and drowning. Some interpreted this to mean that mankind was not meant to fly. Biologically, certainly our bodies are not made to fly, at least not on our own, and thus this is indeed a constraint, and yet we have overcome the constraint by utilizing the Wright Brothers invention to fly via artificial means (I'm writing this right now at 30,000 feet, flying across the United States, in a modern day commercial jet, even though I was not made to fly per se).

In computer science and AI, we deal with constraints in a multitude of ways. When you are mathematically calculating something, there are constraints that you might apply to the formulas that you are using. Optimization is a popular constraint. You might desire to figure something out and want to do so in an optimal way. You decide to impose a constraint that means that you if are able to figure out something, the most optimum version is the best. One person might develop a computer program that takes hours to calculate pi to thousands of digits in size, while someone else writes a program that can do so in minutes, and thus the more optimal one is perhaps preferred.

When my children were young, I'd look in their crayon box and pull out four of the crayons, let's say I selected yellow, red, blue, and green, thus choosing four different colors. I'd then give them a printed map of the world and ask them to use the four colors to colorize the countries and their states or sub-entities as shown on map. They could use whichever of the four colors and do so in whatever manner they desired.

They might opt to color all of North American countries and their sub-entities in green, and perhaps all of Europe's in blue. This would be an easy way to colorize the map. It wouldn't take them very long to do so. They might or might not even choose to use all four of the colors.

For example, the entire map and all of its countries and sub-entities you could just scrawl in with the red crayon. The only particular constraint was that the only colors you could use had to be one or more of the four colors that I had selected.

Let's recast the map coloring problem.

I would add an additional constraint to my children's effort to color the printed map. I would tell them that they were to use the four selected crayons and could not have any entity border that touched another entity border using the same color. For those of you versed in computer science or mathematics, you might recognize this as the infamous four-color conjecture problem that was first promulgated by Francis Guthrie (he mentioned it to his brother, and his brother mentioned it to a college mathematics professor, and eventually it caught the attention of the London Mathematical Society and became a grand problem to be solved).

Coloring maps is interesting, but even more so is the aspect that you can change your perspective to assert that the four-color problem should be applied to algebraic graphs. You might say that the map coloring led to spurring attention to algorithms that could do nifty things with graphs. With the development of chromatic polynomials, you can count how many ways a graph can be colored, using as a parameter the number of distinct colors that you have in-hand.

Anyway, my children delighted in my adding the four-color constraint, in the sense that it made the map coloring problem more challenging. I suppose when I say they were delighted, I should add that they expressed frustration too, since the problem went from very easy to suddenly becoming quite hard.

Furthermore, at first, they assumed that the problem would be easy, since it had been easy to use the colors in whatever fashion they desired, and they thought that with four crayons that the four-color constraints would likewise be simple. They discovered otherwise as they used up many copies of the printed map, trying to arrive at a solution that met the constraint.

There are so-called "hard" constraints and "soft" constraints. Some people confuse the word "hard" with the idea that if the problem itself becomes hard that the constraint that caused it is considered a "hard" constraint. That's not what is meant though by the proper definition of "hard" and "soft" constraints.

A "hard" constraint is considered a constraint that is inflexible. It is imperative. You cannot try to shake it off. You cannot try to bend it to become softer. A "soft" constraint is one that is considered flexible and you can bend it. It is not considered mandatory.

For my children and their coloring of the map, when I added the four-color constraint, I tried to make it seem like a fun game and wanted to see how they might do. After some trial-and-error of using just four colors and getting stuck trying to color the map as based on the constraint that no two borders could have the same color, one of them opted to reach into the crayon bin and pull out another crayon. When I asked what was up with this, I was told that the problem would be easier to solve if it allowed for five colors instead of four.

This was interesting since they accepted the constraint that no two borders could be the same color but had then opted to see if they could loosen the constraint about how many crayon colors could be used. I appreciated the thinking outside-of-the box approach but said that the four-color option was the only option and that using five colors was not allowed in this case. It was considered a "hard" constraint in that it wasn't flexible and could not be altered. Though, I did urge that they might try using five colors as an initial exploration, seeking to to try and figure out how to ultimately reduce things down to just four colors.

From a cognition viewpoint, notice that they accepted one of the "hard" constraints, namely about two borders rule, but tried to stretch one of the other constraints, the number of colors allowed. Since I had not emphasized that the map must be colored with only four colors, it was handy that they tested the waters to make sure that the number of colors allowed was indeed a firm or hard constraint.

In other words, I had handed them only four colors, and one might assume therefore they could only use four colors, but it was certainly worthwhile asking about it, since trying to solve the map problem with just four colors is a lot harder than with five colors.

This brings us to topic of self-imposed constraints, and particularly ones that might be undue.

When I was a professor and taught AI and computer science classes, I used to have my students try to solve the classic problem of a getting items across a river or lake. You've probably heard or seen the problem in various variants. It goes something like this. You are on one side of the river and have with you a fox, a chicken, and some corn. They are currently supervised by you and remain separated from each other. The fox would like to eat the chicken, and the chicken would like to eat the corn.

You have a boat that you can use to get to the other side of the river. You can only take two items with you on each trip. When you reach the other side, you can leave the items there. Any items on that other side can also be taken back to the side that you came from. You want to end-up with all of the three items intact on the other side.

Here's the dilemma. If you take over the chicken and the corn, the moment that you head back to get the fox, the chicken will gladly eat the corn. Fail! If you take over the fox and the chicken, the moment you head back to get the corn, the fox will gleefully eat the chicken. Fail! And so on.

How do you solve this problem?

I won't be a spoiler and tell you how it is solved, and only offer the hint that it involves multiple trips. The reason I bring up the problem is that nearly every time I presented this problem to the students, they had great difficulty solving it because they made an assumption that the least number of trips was a requirement or constraint.

I never said that the number of trips was a constraint. I never said that the boat couldn't go back-and-forth as many times as you desired. This was not a constraint that I had placed on the solution to the problem. I tell you this because if you try to simultaneously solve the problem and also add a self-imposed constraint that the number of trips must be a minimal number, you get yourself into quite a bind trying to solve the problem.

It is not surprising that computer science students would make such an assumption, since they are continually confronted with having to find the most optimal way to solve things. In their beginning algorithm theories classes and programming classes, they usually are asked to write a sorting program. The program is supposed to sort some set of data elements, perhaps a collection of words are to be sorted into alphabetical order. They are likely graded on how efficient their sorting program is. The fastest version that takes the least number of sorting steps is often given the higher grade. This gets them into the mindset that optimality is desired.

Don't get me wrong that somehow I am eschewing optimality. Love it. I'm just saying that it can lead to a kind of cognitive blindness to solving problems. If each new problem that you try to solve, you approach it with the mindset that you must at first shot also always arrive at optimality, you are going to have a tough road in life, I would wager.

There are times that you should try to solve a problem in whatever way possible, and then afterwards try to wean it down to make it optimal. Trying to do two things at once, solving a problem and doing so optimally, can be too big a chunk of food to swallow all in one bite.

Problems that are of interest to computer scientists and AI specialists are often labeled as Constraint Satisfaction Problems (CSP's). These are problems for which there are some number of constraints that need to be abided by, or satisfied, as part of the solution that you are seeking. For my children, it was the constraint that they had to use the map I provided, they could not allow the same color to touch one border and another border, and they must use only the four colors.

Notice there were multiple constraints. They were all considered "hard" constraints in that I wouldn't let them flex any of the constraints. This is classic CSP.

I did somewhat flex the number of colors, but only in the sense that I urged them to try with five colors to get used to trying to do the problem (after they had broached the subject). This is in keeping with my point above that sometimes it is good to solve a problem by loosening a constraint. You might then tighten the constraint after you've already come up with some strategy or tactic that you discovered when you had flexed a constraint.

Some refer to a CSP that contains "soft" constraints as one that is considered Flexible. A classic version of CSP usually states that all of the given constraints are considered hard or inflexible. If you are faced with a problem that does allow for some of the constraints to be flexible, it is referred to as a FCSP (Flexible CSP), meaning there is some flexibility allowed in one or more of the constraints. It does not necessarily mean that all of the constraints are flexible or soft, just that some of them are.

What does this have to do with AI self-driving cars?

At the Cybernetic AI Self-Driving Car Institute, we are developing AI software for self-driving cars. One aspect that deserves apt attention is the self-imposed undue constraints that some AI developers are putting into their AI systems for self-driving cars.

Allow me to elaborate.

I'd like to first clarify and introduce the notion that there are varying levels of AI self-driving cars. The topmost level is considered Level 5. A Level 5 self-driving car is one that is being driven by the AI and there is no human driver involved. For the design of Level 5 self-driving cars, the auto makers are even removing the gas pedal, brake pedal, and steering wheel, since those are contraptions used by human drivers. The Level 5 self-driving car is not being driven by a human and nor is there an expectation that a human driver will be present in the self-driving car. It's all on the shoulders of the AI to drive the car.

For self-driving cars less than a Level 5, there must be a human driver present in the car. The human driver is currently considered the responsible party for the acts of the car. The AI and the human driver are co-sharing the driving task. In spite of this co-sharing, the human is supposed to remain fully immersed into the driving task and be ready at all times to perform the driving task. I've repeatedly warned about the dangers of this co-sharing arrangement and predicted it will produce many untoward results.

Let's focus herein on the true Level 5 self-driving car. Much of the comments apply to the less than Level 5 self-driving cars too, but the fully autonomous AI self-driving car will receive the most attention in this discussion.

Here's the usual steps involved in the AI driving task:
- Sensor data collection and interpretation
- Sensor fusion
- Virtual world model updating
- AI action planning
- Car controls command issuance

Another key aspect of AI self-driving cars is that they will be driving on our roadways in the midst of human driven cars too. There are some pundits of AI self-driving cars that continually refer to a utopian world in which there are only AI self-driving cars on the public roads. Currently there are about 250+ million conventional cars in the United States alone, and those cars are not going to magically disappear or become true Level 5 AI self-driving cars overnight.

Indeed, the use of human driven cars will last for many years, likely many decades, and the advent of AI self-driving cars will occur while there are still human driven cars on the roads. This is a crucial point since this means that the AI of self-driving cars needs to be able to contend with not just other AI self-driving cars, but also contend with human driven cars. It is easy to envision a simplistic and rather unrealistic world in which all AI self-driving cars are politely interacting with each other and being civil about roadway interactions. That's not what is going to be happening for the foreseeable future. AI self-driving cars and human driven cars will need to be able to cope with each other.

Returning to the topic of self-imposed undue constraints, let's consider how this applies to AI self-driving cars.

I'll provide some examples of driving behavior that exhibit the self-imposed undue constraints phenomena. Keep in mind my earlier story about the computer science students that attempted to solve the river crossing problem and did so with the notion of optimality permeating their minds, which made it much harder to solve the problem.

It was a rainy day and I was trying to get home before the rain completely flooded the streets around my domicile. Though in Southern California we don't get much rain, maybe a dozen inches a year, whenever we do get rain it seems like our gutters and flood-control are not built to handle it. Plus, the drivers here go nuts when there is rain. In most other rain-familiar cities, the drivers take rain in stride. Here, drivers get freaked out.

You would think they would drive more slowly and carefully. It seems to be the opposite, namely in rain they drive more recklessly and with abandon.

I was driving down a street that definitely was somewhat flooded. The water was gushing around the sides of my car as I proceeded forward. I slowed down quite a bit. Unfortunately, I found myself almost driving into a kind of watery quicksand. As I proceeded forward, the water got deeper and deeper. I realized too late that the water was now nearly up to the doors of my car. I wondered what would happen once the water was up to the engine and whether it might conk out the engine. I also was worried that the water would seep into the car and I'd have a nightmare of a flooded interior to deal with.

I looked in my rearview mirror and considered trying to back out of the situation by going in reverse. Unfortunately, other cars had followed me and they were blocking me from behind. As I rounded a bend, I could see ahead of me that several cars had gotten completed stranded in the water up ahead. This was a sure sign that I was heading into deeper waters and likely also would get stuck.

Meanwhile, one of those pick-up trucks with a high clearance went past me going fast, splashing a torrent of water onto my car. He was gunning it to make it through the deep waters. Probably was the type that had gotten ribbed about having such a truck for suburbs and why he bought such a monster, and here was his one moment to relish the purchase. Yippee, I think he was exclaiming.

I then saw one car ahead of me that did something I would never have likely considered. He drove up onto the median of the road. There was a raised median that divided the north bound and south bound lanes. It was a grassy median that was raised up to the height of the sidewalk, maybe an inch or two higher. By driving up onto the median, the driver ahead of me had gotten almost entirely out of the water, though there were some parts of the median that were flooded and underwater. In any case, it was a viable means of escape.

I had just enough traction left on the road surface to urge my car up onto the median. I then drove on the median until I reached a point that would allow me to come off it and head down a cross-street that was not so flooded. As I did so, I looked back at the other cars that were mired in the flooded street that I had just left. They were getting out of their cars and I could see water pouring from the interiors. What a mess!

Why do I tell this tale of woe and survival (well, Okay, not real survival in that I wasn't facing the grim reaper, just a potentially stranded car that would be flooded and require lots of effort to ultimately get out of the water and then deal with the flooded interior)?

As a law-abiding driver, I would never have considered driving up on the median of a road. It just wouldn't occur to me. In my mind, it was verboten. The median is off-limits. You could get a ticket for driving on the median. It was something only scofflaws would do. It was a constraint that was part of my driving mindset. Never drive on a median.

In that sense, it was a "hard" constraint. If you had asked me before the flooding situation whether I would ever drive on a median, I am pretty sure I would have said no. I considered it inviolate. It was so ingrained in my mind that even when I saw another driver ahead of me do it, for a split second I rejected the approach, merely due to my conditioning that driving on the median was wrong and was never to be undertaken.

I look back at it now and realize that I should have classified the constraint as a "soft" constraint. Most of the time, you probably should not be driving on the median. That seems to be a relatively fair notion. There might be though conditions under which you can flex the constraint and can drive on the median. My flooding situation seemed to be that moment.

Let's now recast this constraint in light of AI self-driving cars. Should an AI self-driving car ever be allowed to drive up onto the median and drive on the median?

I've inspected and reviewed some of the AI software being used in open source for self-driving cars and it contains constraints that prohibit such a driving act from ever occurring. It is verboten by the software.

I would say it is a self-imposed undue constraint.

Sure, we don't want AI self-driving cars willy nilly driving on medians. That would be dangerous and potentially horrific. Does this mean that the constrain though must be "hard" and inflexible? Does it mean that there might not ever be a circumstance in which an AI system would "rightfully" opt to drive on the median? I'm sure that in addition to my escape of flooding, we could come up with other bona fide reasons that a car might want or need to drive on a median.

I realize that you might be concerned that driving on the median should be a human judgement aspect and not be made by some kind of automation such as the AI system that's driving an AI self-driving car. This raises other thorny elements. If a human passenger commands the AI self-driving car to drive on a median, does that ergo mean that the AI should abide by such a command? I doubt we want that to occur, since you could have a human passenger that is wacko that commands their AI self-driving car to drive onto a median, doing so for either no reason or for a nefarious reason.

I assert that there are lots of these kinds of currently hidden constraints in many of the AI self-driving cars that are being experimented with in trials today on our public roadways. The question will be whether ultimately these self-imposed undue or "hard" constraints will limit the advent of true AI self-driving cars.

To me, an AI self-driving car that cannot figure out how to get out of a flooded street by driving up onto the median is not a true AI self-driving car.

I realize this sets a pretty high bar. I mention this too because there were many other human drivers on that street that either did not think of the possibility or thought of the possibility after it was too late to try and maneuver onto the median. If some humans cannot come up with a solution, are we asking too much for the AI to come up with a solution?

In my case, I freely admit that it was not my own idea to drive up on the median. I saw someone else do it and then weighed whether I should do the same. In that manner, you could suggest that I had in that moment learned something new about driving. After all these many years of driving, and perhaps I thought I had learned it all, in that flooded street I was suddenly shocked awake into the realization that I could drive on the median. Of course, I had always known it was possible, the thing that was stopping me was the mindset that it was out-of-bounds and never to be considered as a viable place to drive my car.

For AI self-driving cars, it is anticipated that via Machine Learning (ML) and Deep Learning (DL) they will be able to gradually over time develop more and more in their driving skills. You might say that I learned that driving on the median was a possibility and viable in an emergency situation such as a flooded street. Would the AI of an AI self-driving car be able to learn the same kind of aspect?

The "hard" constraints inside much of the AI systems for self-driving cars is embodied in a manner that it is typically not allowed to be revised. The ML and DL takes place for other aspects of the self-driving car, such as "learning" about new roads or new paths to go when driving the self-driving car. Doing ML or DL on the AI action planning portions is still relatively untouched territory. It would pretty much require a human AI developer to go into the AI system and soften the constraint of driving on a median, rather than the AI itself doing some kind of introspective analysis and changing itself accordingly.

There's another aspect regarding much of today's state-of-the-art on ML and DL that would make it difficult to have done what I did in terms of driving up onto the median. For most ML and DL, you need to have available lots and lots of examples for the ML or DL to pattern match onto. After examining thousands or maybe millions of instances of pictures of road signs, the ML or DL can somewhat differentiate stop signs versus say yield signs.

When I was on the flooded street, it took only one instance for me to learn to overcome my prior constraint about not driving on the median. I saw one car do it. I then generalized that if one car could do so, perhaps other cars could. I then figured out that my car could do the same. I then enacted this. All of that took place based on just one example. And in a split second of time. And within the confines of my car.

It happened based on one example and occurred within my car, which is significant to highlight. For the Machine Learning of AI self-driving cars, most of the auto makers and tech firms are currently restricting any ML to occur in the cloud. Via OTA (Over-The-Air) electronic communications, an AI self-driving car sends data that it has collected from being on the streets and pushes it up to the cloud. The auto maker or tech firm does some amount of ML or DL via the cloud-based data, and then creates updates or patches that are pushed down into the AI self-driving car via the OTA.

In the case of my being on the flooded street, suppose that I was in an AI self-driving car. Suppose that the AI via its sensors could detect that a car up ahead went up onto the median. And assume too that the sensors detected that the street was getting flooded. Would the on-board AI have been able to make the same kind of mental leap, learning from the one instance, and adjust itself, all on-board the AI of the self-driving car? Today, likely no.

I'm sure some AI developers are saying that if the self-driving car had OTA it could have pushed the data up to the cloud and then a patch or update might have been pumped back into the self-driving car, allowing the AI to then go up onto the median. Really?

Consider that I would have to be in a place that allowed for the OTA to function (since it is electronic communication, it won't always have a clear signal). Consider that the cloud system would have to be dealing with this data and tons of other data coming from many other self-driving cars. Consider that the pumping down of the patch would have to be done immediately and be put into use immediately, since time was a crucial element. Etc. Not likely.

At this juncture, you might be tempted to say that I've only given one example of a "hard" constraint in a driving task and it is maybe rather obscure. So what if an AI self-driving car could not discern the value of driving onto the median. This might happen once in a blue moon, and you might say that it would be safer to have the "hard" constraint than to not have it in place (I'm not saying that such a constraint should not be in place, and instead arguing that it needs to be a "soft" constraint that can be flexed in the right way at the right time for the right reasons).

Here's another driving story for you that might help.

I was driving on a highway that was in an area prone to wildfires. Here in Southern California (SoCal) we occasionally have wildfires, especially during the summer months when the brush is dry and there is a lot of tinder ready to go up in flames. The mass media news often makes it seem as though all of SoCal gets caught up in such wildfires. The reality is that it tends to be localized. That being said, the air can get pretty brutal once the wildfires get going and large plumes of smoke can be seen for miles.

Driving along on this highway in an area known for wildfires, I could see up ahead that there was smoke filling the air. I hoped that the highway would skirt around the wildfires and I could just keep driving until I got past it. I neared a tunnel and there was some smoke filling into it. There wasn't any nearby exits to get off the highway. The tunnel still had enough visibility that I thought I could zip through the tunnel and pop out the other side safely. I'd driven through this tunnel on many other trips and knew that at my speed of 65 miles per hour it would not take long to traverse the tunnel.

Upon entering into the tunnel, I realize it was a mistake to do so. Besides the smoke, when I neared the other end of the tunnel, there were flames reaching out across the highway and essentially blocking the highway up ahead. This tunnel was a one-way. Presumably, I could not go back in the same direction as I had just traversed. If I tried to get out of the tunnel, it looked like I might get my car caught into the fire.

Fortunately, all of the cars that had entered into the tunnel had grinded to a near halt or at least a very low speed. The drivers all realized the danger of trying to dash out of the tunnel. I saw one or two cars make the try. I later found out they did get some scorching by the fire. There were other cars that ended-up on the highway and the drivers abandoned their cars due to the flames. Several of those cars got completely burned to a crisp.

In any case, we all made U-turns there in the tunnel and headed in the wrong direction of the tunnel so that we could drive out and get back to the safer side of the tunnel.

Would an AI self-driving car be able and willing to drive the wrong-way on a highway? Again, most of the AI self-driving cars today would not allow it. They are coded to prevent such a thing from happening. We can all agree that having an AI system drive a self-driving car the wrong-way on a road is generally undesirable. Should it though be a "hard" constraint that is never allowed to soften? I think not.

As another story, I'll make this quick, I was driving on the freeway and a dog happened to scamper onto the road. The odds were high that a car was going to ram into the dog. The dog was frightened out of its wits and was running back-and-forth wantonly. Some of the drivers didn't seem to care and were just wanting to drive past the dog, perhaps rushing on their way to work or to get their Starbucks morning coffee.

I then saw something that was heartwarming. Maybe a bit dangerous, but nonetheless heartwarming. Several cars appeared to coordinate with each other to slow down the traffic (they slowed down and got the cars behind them to do the same) and brought traffic to a halt. They then maneuvered their cars to make a kind of fence or kennel surrounding the dog. This prevented the dog from readily running away. Some of the drivers then got out of their cars and one had a leash (presumably a dog owner), leashed the dog, got the dog into their car, and drove away, along with the rest of traffic resuming.

Would an AI self-driving car have been able to do this same kind of act, specifically coming to a halt on the freeway and turning the car kitty corner while on the freeway to help make the shape of the virtual fence?

This would likely violate other self-imposed constraints that the AI has embodied into it. Doubtful that today's AI could have aided in this rescue effort.

In case you still think these are all oddball edge cases, let's consider other kinds of potential AI constraints that likely exist for self-driving cars, as put in place by the AI developers involved. What about going faster than the speed limit? I've had some AI developers say that they've setup the system so that the self-driving car will never go faster than the posted speed limit. I'd say that we can come up with lots of reasons why at some point a self-driving car might want or need to go faster than the posted speed limit.

Indeed, I've said and written many times that the notion that an AI self-driving car is never going to do any kind of "illegal" driving is nonsense. It is a simplistic viewpoint that defies what actually driving consists of.

Conclusion

The nature of constraints is that we could not live without them, and nor at times can we live with them, or at least that's what many profess to say.

For AI systems, it is important to be aware of the kinds of constraints they are being hidden or hard-coded into them, along with understanding which of the constraints are hard and inflexible, and which ones are soft and flexible.

It is a dicey proposition to have soft constraints. I say this because for each of my earlier examples in which a constraint was flexed, I gave examples wherein the flexing was considered appropriate.

Suppose though that the AI is poorly able to discern when to flex a soft constraint and when not to do so?

Today's AI is so brittle and incapable that we are likely better off to have hard constraints and deal with those consequences, rather than having soft constraints that could be handy in some instances but maybe disastrous in other instances.

To achieve a true AI self-driving car, I claim that the constraints must nearly all be "soft" and that the AI needs to discern when to appropriately bend them.

This does not mean that the AI can do so arbitrarily. This also takes us into the realm of the ethics of AI self-driving cars. Who is to decide when the AI can and cannot flex those soft constraints?

My children have long moved on from the four-color crayon mapping problem and they are faced nowadays with the daily reality of constraints all around them as adults.

The AI of today that is driving self-driving cars is at best the capability of a young child, which is well-below where we need to be in terms of having AI systems that are responsible for multi-ton cars that can wreak havoc and cause damage and injury.

Let's at least make sure that we are aware of the internal self-imposed constraints embedded in AI systems and whether or not the AI might be blind to taking appropriate action while driving on our roads. That's the kind of undue that we need to undue before it is too late.

CHAPTER 7

ALIEN LIMB SYNDROME

AND

AI SELF-DRIVING CARS

CHAPTER 7

ALIEN LIMB SYNDROME

AND

AI SELF-DRIVING CARS

Their hands did it. That's what my children told me when they were quite young and had managed to put their hands onto wet paint. We had been taking a leisurely stroll in our quiet neighborhood and a homeowner had opted to paint his wooden picket fence that bordered his property. There was a sign that clearly said wet paint that had been posted on the fence. As we got near to the property, I asked the kids what the sign said. They both knew just enough about how to read that they were able to decipher the sign and tell me what it indicated. Case closed, or so I thought.

I had wandered just slightly ahead of the kids and assumed that they were walking behind me, straight as an arrow, and I took no qualm that they might decide to put their hands onto that freshly painted picket fence. When they caught up with me, I happened to see them both hiding their arms and hands. What's up, I asked, not having yet put two and two together, so to speak.

They knew that I would be a bit perturbed about their getting paint onto their hands and so they first tried the hideaway technique. Since I had now asked to essentially see their hands, they were somewhat stuck in terms of what to do. One of them showed me the paint on their hands and claimed that the posted sign did not say "Don't Touch" and only said wet paint was there. How were they supposed to know not to touch it?

Though I appreciated the clever semantics lesson, it didn't cut mustard with me. When I gave them my classic evil eye, the other one tried an entirely different approach. Our hands did it, I was curtly informed. How's that, I inquired?

Well, both them opted to chime in simultaneously now and professed that it was an act performed by their hands. They had no control over their hands. Somehow, magically, mysteriously, their hands had decided on their own to touch that paint, without consulting with the rest of their bodies and mind, and that's how it happened.

I suppose that I could have played along and said that therefore their hands would suffer the consequences, but I figured this whole transgression was rather mild and probably best to let it go as a lesson about not touching wet paint. They hadn't ever touched wet paint like this before, as far as I knew. Sure, they had used paints in school and at our home they painted quite a bit. I don't recall them though ever getting paint onto their hands at any other location.

When we got home, I asked them if they had regained sufficient control of their hands that they could go wash off the paint from their hands. They nodded their heads in agreement that somehow they once again were in direct control of their hands. Off they went, rubbing paint remover on their skin and washing their hands. It's a funny story now and one that I remember vividly, while they today as young adults don't remember it at all.

What makes the story particularly notable too is that they unknowingly landed on an actual aliment that exists. There is a phenomenon of people that are unable to control their limbs. It is typically referred to as alien limb syndrome. My kids didn't actually have it.

I'll say this, if they could have quoted me the name of the ailment and said it was alien limb syndrome, I would have likely not only considered the wet paint a non-issue but would have gotten them ice cream as a reward for knowing a rather obscure malady at their exceedingly young age.

For those of you that are movie buffs, you might remember that in the movie Dr. Strangelove the main fictional character is unable to control his arm and hand, and he flails them uncontrollably around at times, making the character seem grotesque and befitting with the role. We ought to though not consider the movie as any kind of supporter for considering this as a serious ailment and a medical condition that we should give careful and due consideration for.

Some people even refer to the alien limb syndrome as the Dr. Strangelove syndrome. There are also some that refer to this aliment as the alien hand syndrome, though the condition can impact arms, legs, feet, and essentially all of the limbs. It is not exclusively for the hands, though the hand as the focus does seem to be the more popular affected limb (for those of us left handed, spookily it also seems to be primarily the left hand!).

The uncontrollable limb movements can at times be quite subtle. There are online videos that you can watch and show someone afflicted with alien limb syndrome that suddenly buttons their sweater. They do so without apparently wanting to do so. The person claims they did not have a thought in their head about buttoning their sweater. Their arms and hands just decided to do so. Moments later, after having buttoned up, their arms and hands proceed to unbutton the sweater. No rhyme, nor reason, appears to have prompted it.

Is the person trying to fool with us? Maybe they really did have thoughts about buttoning and unbuttoning their sweater. Perhaps they want us to belief they didn't think it to happen. If we put aside someone that is purposely trying to scam us, I'd say that it does seem realistic that the person truly believed they did not actively invoke their brain to do the buttoning and unbuttoning act.

Of course, we can't know for sure what is happening in the person's brain. Maybe a part of their brain told their arms and hands to do the act, while another part of the brain was unaware that the other part was acting to do so. It could be that the person is only aware of the part of the brain that was unaware and so they tell us that their brain did not command their arms and hands.

Some assert that alien limb syndrome is a disentanglement of the mind and the body. The limbs genuinely are acting on their own. The mind is not involved at all. There tends to be less credence to support this notion. Some say that the disentanglement is within the mind, causing parts of the mind to become disentangled, such as the part that controls the motor functions of the limbs and the part that does action planning for the body.

Another intriguing element of the alien limb syndrome is that sometimes one limb will seemingly try to purposely counteract the other limb. This commonly occurs when one disobedient limb tries to do something and another disobedient limb tries to then intervene. Let's say the left arm and left hand are wayward. The left arm and left hand start to button up the sweater. The right arm and right hand might suddenly come up to the left arm and left hand and attempt to stop the buttoning process, even though they too are seemingly uncontrolled by the person. Or, once the buttoning has been completed, the right arm and right hand might immediately unbutton the sweater, rather than trying to directly fight with the other mind-of-its-own limb.

Imagine for a moment that one or more of your limbs exhibited this alien limb syndrome. I'd wager that it would certainly freak you out. We are all accustomed to the idea that we control our limbs. There are times that we suddenly become aware of our limbs as somewhat distinct appendages, such as if you fall asleep on your arm and hand, and it begins to tingle, doing so on its own. You've perhaps flapped your sleeping hand and arm to get it to awaken and felt like your limb was a limp noodle that you had no real control over.

The people that get alien limb syndrome are likely to gradually get somewhat accustomed to the matter, though it is not an easy thing to deal with. The person will at times speak to their alien limb and try to talk it into submission. They might even give a name to the limb, as though it has its own personality. They can often tell you generally when their limb is going to act up, having dealt with it for a while and know the kinds of acts that the limb tries to do on its own.

There are obviously dangers involved in having the alien limb syndrome. Suppose your limb acts up when you least want it to do so. Maybe you are holding a pair of scissors and all of a sudden the disobedient limb opts to strike you or someone else. The person with the alien limb syndrome would say they had no control over their limb and it wasn't their doing per se.

If you are interested in the alien limb syndrome, there are lots of fascinating studies trying to pin down what cause it and what can be done about it. In a recent study done at Vanderbilt University, researchers seemed to trace the aliment to connections in the brain involving the precuneus. The precuneus is often considered the part of the brain that provides our sense of free will and what is coined our agency.

One key aspect of the study was that there didn't seem to be one specific area of the brain that could be considered the culprit for the syndrome. Some have been hoping that the matter is isolated to a particular spot of the brain and thus it would presumably be easier to detect and resolve. This recent study suggests it is more broadly based and involves a network of regions of the brain. Generally, it seems to be the case that whenever neurologists and others that study the brain are hoping to pinpoint the brain on some matter, it usually becomes more complex and seemingly is distributed throughout the brain. No single silver bullet, so to speak.

As a seasoned AI developer and software engineer, I've had situations involving computer systems that in some analogous way appeared to have been overtaken by an alien limb syndrome.

I remember one time that I was involved in creating a rather complex piece of software that had lots of components. Some of the software routines had been found in open source libraries. One of the routines was purportedly built to calculate multi-dimensional scales for doing pattern matching. A member of the software team tried playing with it and said it would do what we needed to have done. It then got included into our overall build of the system.

Things worked fine for a while. One day, we received a complaint that our system was trying to access files that were outside the scope of the system. Which element of the hundreds of components was the culprit? At first, nobody knew and all the members of the software team claimed it could not be any of their components.

For various reasons, we had a hard time finding the culprit. We could not readily replicate the problem and we didn't have much in the way of clues from the complaint that had been registered. Some of the team felt like we were barking up a wrong tree and that it must be something occurring outside of our system, rather than something inside of our system.

As you might guess, the darned thing happened again and we got a new complaint about a file being accessed that should not have been. Once is maybe a fluke, twice seems to suggest a rogue element that won't just disappear on its own.

After turning over all possible rocks and stones, we eventually narrowed the matter to the open source routine that we had used. Sure enough, hidden deep inside it, we found a few lines of code that did not especially belong there. It didn't seem to be malicious and maybe was leftover from some other functionality that the original developers had in mind to include but had later tried to excise it, doing so incompletely.

In a manner of speaking, we had an alien limb syndrome. One of the "limbs" of the core system had gone alien on us.

The core system wasn't doing it. The limb was acting on its own. We did "surgery" on the limb and put in back into proper operation. Perhaps someday the same kind of action can be taken for humans that experience alien limb syndrome. Let's hope so.

What does this have to do with AI self-driving cars?

At the Cybernetic AI Self-Driving Car Institute, we are developing AI software for self-driving cars. One aspect that AI developers generally should be doing is building their systems to catch and prevent an alien limb syndrome from overtaking the rest of their AI system.

This is especially crucial in a real-time system and really especially so in a real-time system that controls a self-driving car -- there can be serious life-or-death consequences for an "alien limb" acting up in an AI self-driving car.

Allow me to elaborate.

I'd like to first clarify and introduce the notion that there are varying levels of AI self-driving cars. The topmost level is considered Level 5. A Level 5 self-driving car is one that is being driven by the AI and there is no human driver involved. For the design of Level 5 self-driving cars, the auto makers are even removing the gas pedal, brake pedal, and steering wheel, since those are contraptions used by human drivers. The Level 5 self-driving car is not being driven by a human and nor is there an expectation that a human driver will be present in the self-driving car. It's all on the shoulders of the AI to drive the car.

For self-driving cars less than a Level 5, there must be a human driver present in the car. The human driver is currently considered the responsible party for the acts of the car. The AI and the human driver are co-sharing the driving task. In spite of this co-sharing, the human is supposed to remain fully immersed into the driving task and be ready at all times to perform the driving task. I've repeatedly warned about the dangers of this co-sharing arrangement and predicted it will produce many untoward results.

Let's focus herein on the true Level 5 self-driving car. Much of the comments apply to the less than Level 5 self-driving cars too, but the fully autonomous AI self-driving car will receive the most attention in this discussion.

Here's the usual steps involved in the AI driving task:
- Sensor data collection and interpretation
- Sensor fusion
- Virtual world model updating
- AI action planning
- Car controls command issuance

Another key aspect of AI self-driving cars is that they will be driving on our roadways in the midst of human driven cars too. There are some pundits of AI self-driving cars that continually refer to a utopian world in which there are only AI self-driving cars on the public roads. Currently there are about 250+ million conventional cars in the United States alone, and those cars are not going to magically disappear or become true Level 5 AI self-driving cars overnight.

Indeed, the use of human driven cars will last for many years, likely many decades, and the advent of AI self-driving cars will occur while there are still human driven cars on the roads. This is a crucial point since this means that the AI of self-driving cars needs to be able to contend with not just other AI self-driving cars, but also contend with human driven cars. It is easy to envision a simplistic and rather unrealistic world in which all AI self-driving cars are politely interacting with each other and being civil about roadway interactions. That's not what is going to be happening for the foreseeable future. AI self-driving cars and human driven cars will need to be able to cope with each other.

Returning to the topic of alien limb syndrome in complex computer-based systems, savvy AI developers need to be on their toes and build their AI systems to cope with alien limbs that might act up.

Let's start with the potential of the sensors to become one or more alien limbs.

Suppose one of the cameras on an AI self-driving car starts to go rogue. Rather than providing images at a particular pace as established by the AI system, the camera instead begins to generate tons of images. Maybe it opts to also provide them on a seeming whim, doing so intermittently or perhaps even incessantly. This could lead to either a flood of images that the AI system was not anticipating or a dearth of images and cause a kind of visual starvation.

If the rest of the AI system is not prepared in-advance to handle this kind of alien limb activity, it could cause quite a problem. The AI effort to make sense of the images as to whether there is a car ahead or a pedestrian in the way might be marred by getting the images on such an unexpected basis. If the AI is fooled into believing what the camera is providing, it could lead to an internal cascading set of errors and confusion.

For example, during sensor fusion, if we assume that say the radar and LIDAR are still functioning properly, there will now be a potential contention between what the camera indicates and what those other sensors indicate. Which of the sensors is to be believed by the AI? If the AI falsely assumes that the camera is correct, it could attempt to override the radar and LIDAR, or might give the radar and LIDAR less weight in trying to ascertain the surroundings.

Suppose that the miscues then were passed along to the updates of the virtual world model. Maybe the virtual world model places a marker that there is a pedestrian on the sidewalk when the actual fact is the pedestrian is standing in the street. When the AI action planning kicks in, it will inspect the virtual world model and falsely get an indication that there isn't a pedestrian in the way. The AI action planning might opt to issue car commands that tell the self-driving car to continue forward at the ongoing speed, even though the self-driving car is now moving closer and closer to hitting the pedestrian that's in the street.

I realize that some AI developers might complain about the aforementioned scenario and would assert that even the simplest of sensors on an AI self-driving car are bound to have some kind of built-in error checking. Thus, those AI developers would say that certainly the sensor itself would be reporting errors and this would give the sensor data collector and the sensor fusion a heads-up that the camera is defective.

Though this is indeed the case that the sensors are likely to have error detection, I'd like to also point out that whether or not the error detection can detect rogue behavior is another kind of matter. In other words, the error detection for most sensors would be that the camera is not working at all, maybe due to having encountered an outright hardware failure or maybe it got smacked by a piece of debris that flew up from the street and cracked or broke the camera.

In the alien limb syndrome notion, I'm saying that let's assume the camera is otherwise working just fine and it is now working on its own and not necessarily at the command of the rest of the AI system.

In that manner, the error detection by the sensor itself might not even realize that the sensor has gone rogue. The usual error detection involves that the sensor has blurry images or no images, while I'm suggesting in the alien limb manner the images are overall fine. This is the same as when a human with alien limb syndrome suddenly has their arm and hand act up, namely that the arm and hand are working as an arm and a hand and there is nothing wrong with those appendages per se (i.e., the arm still extends, the hand still grasps), and they function as an arm and a hand are expected.

It is imperative that the AI be prepared for realizing that a sensor, any of the sensors, might suddenly go rogue. This is a tough aspect to figure out because let's assume that the sensor is still fully functioning in terms of whatever the sensor is capable of doing. If it is a camera, we are still getting good camera images. If it is a radar, we are still getting solid radar returns. The problem is that this sensor is doing its sensory acts whenever it opts to do them, rather than upon the command of the AI system.

It might involve other functionality of the sensor too. For example, suppose the camera can be automatically adjusted to focus on nearby objects or far away objects. Let's suppose that the AI has recently set the camera on the far away focus. During the rogue action, the camera might on its own switch into the nearby focus and provide those images. The AI was expecting far away images and meanwhile it suddenly gets nearby images. Would the AI be able to detect this? That's the million-dollar question, as they say.

The other complication is that the rogue act might be fleeting rather than consistent. In the case of humans, the aspect of suddenly buttoning a sweater can occur out-of-the-blue. It might happen and then not happen again for a long time. Or, it might happen and then happen again, and again, and again.

The case of the consistently being rogue is probably going to be easier for the AI system to realize that something is amiss. Something that happens intermittently is likely to be more challenging to discern. It is akin to my earlier story about the open source subroutine that we had used in our system and it croaked once and then get silent after that, otherwise working as it was supposed to do. Those kinds of oddball acts are often more difficult to ferret out.

Detecting the alien limb is crucial. Having a means to deal with the detected rogue acts is equally crucial. If a flood of images are pouring in, the AI would need to ascertain which images to keep and which to potentially discard. You might be thinking that shouldn't it analyze all of the images received? Well, keep in mind that as a real-time system it takes time for the system to analyze each image, and it could be that the system will fall behind if it merely opts to analyze every image being flooded into the system.

Imagine that the flood caused a backlog of the image analyzer. Meanwhile, the self-driving car is still moving ahead. The delay in the sensor analysis of the backlog might mean that a few crucial seconds are lost that might have made the difference in terms of the AI action planner realizing that the self-driving car is going ram into a pedestrian or another car.

In short, there is a chance that any of the sensors might become an alien limb. This could happen to just one of the sensors or it could occur to more than one. It could be that one sensor acts up and then seems to settle down, or it could be that several act up at once (many limbs). I mention these multitude of variations because the AI system cannot just assume that if there is an alien limb it will be neatly confined to just one sensor. That would be too easy. The real-world won't necessarily make things easy for the AI.

Beyond the sensors, an alien limb can strike other aspects of the AI self-driving car system. Perhaps the sensor fusion goes rogue. Maybe the virtual world model goes rogue and starts populating the model with all sorts of markers that aren't based on what the sensors and sensor fusion have reported. The AI action planner itself might go rogue. Generally, the deeper within the AI system that the alien limb strikes, the harder it will be to ascertain and deal with.

I've mentioned that the AI system needs to be prepared in-advance for alien limb syndromes that might arise.

Some AI developers might balk at this notion that they need to develop the AI system to cope with rogue behavior and offer instead that the AI system should by itself be able to deal with alien limbs. As an analogy to a human, do we need to tell a human before they get alien limbs that they should be prepared to deal with alien limbs, or instead might we expect that a human that suddenly has alien limbs will be able to cope with it whenever it suddenly so occurs.

Should we relieve the AI developers of the AI system to not have to deal with the possibility of alien limb syndrome and instead assume or hope that the AI system can somehow figure out the aspect on its own?

I'd vote that since we're dealing with an AI self-driving car, and since there is a solid chance that the AI self-driving car could cause undue damage or injury, it makes a lot more sense to prepare the AI system beforehand, rather than hope or assume that the AI will somehow miraculously figure out what to do. This is generally true too of humans in that a human that were to suddenly discover they have alien limb syndrome is likely to be startled and not deal with it very well, and presumably once they see a medical specialist it might be more likely they could work toward behaviors to help contend with it.

There is a slim chance that some kind of Machine Learning (ML) or Deep Learning (DL) capability of the AI system for the self-driving car might be able to identify that something is amiss, and maybe gradually figure out that it is rogue behavior. This might though take many iterations and it is usually the case with today's ML and DL that tons of examples are needed to find patterns. I don't think we want the alien limb acts to mount up and instead want to catch them as soon as they arise, thus, waiting for the off-chance that the ML or DL might catch on is not a good strategy for safety purposes.

Let's now consider and assume that a rightfully developed AI self-driving car has been crafted to be able to detect and contend with alien limb syndrome (I hope so!).

There are some added twists to consider.

One is a false positive effect. The AI might falsely accuse a capability to be suffering from alien limb, and yet perhaps the capability is actually functioning properly and appropriately. The danger is that if the AI has opted to now perhaps disregard the limb or otherwise treat it as suspect, whether it is a sensor or some other component, the AI is doing so falsely.

Let's pretend that a key camera has been accused of being an alien limb. The AI perhaps does something like opting to now ignore whatever the camera provides as data. If the camera is an alien limb, this might be a prudent blockage to prevent flooding and delays on processing of the camera images. But, if the "solution" is merely to ignore the camera, we've also now lost the use of a valuable sensor. Furthermore, if the sensor is not actually experiencing an alien limb syndrome, and yet it has been labeled as such by the AI, we are now neglecting the camera needlessly.

The odds are that any alien limb treatment is bound to degrade the limb and not be using it to its normal full potential. Thus, the AI might be incorrectly now be overriding or wrestling with a component that actually is able to work fine.

The other side of this coin is a false negative indication. The AI might somehow inspect or assess a capability and determine that it is not suffering from an alien limb syndrome, and yet the capability actually is. In other words, we cannot assume that the AI system is going to necessarily always correctly discern when an alien syndrome is occurring.

I say this and it sometimes surprises AI developers, since they tend to get themselves into the mindset that if they've included some kind of alien limb detection, it is going to work flawlessly and all of the time correctly ascertain an alien limb existence. I don't think this is real-world thinking. There are odds that even with a detection purposely built into your AI system, there is a chance that an alien limb might scoot through and the detection will miss catching it.

Conclusion

There are some AI developers that are oblivious to the alien limb syndrome when it comes to their AI systems. It is their assumption that the components of their AI system are going to work correctly and that within them is some kind of self-error checking. Therefore, the rest of the AI system does not need to be concerned about the component because the component itself will let the rest of the AI system know when it is not working properly.

As mentioned, the alien limb syndrome is not particularly about the component itself having errors. An internal self-check would come out usually Okay, indicating that the element is still working properly, similarly to how a hand and arm might be working just fine to button or unbutton a sweater. It is more about the invoking of the component and having it do its thing when desired, as desired, rather than the component opting to run or activate at its own choosing.

For an AI self-driving car, any of the "limbs" of the AI system can wreak havoc if it opts to activate whenever it opts to do so. When I use the word "limb" it tends to bring forth the idea that the sensors of the self-driving car might go rogue, but please realize that as I've mentioned herein, the "limb" is a metaphor referring to any of the components of the AI system, including the sensors, sensor fusion, virtual world model, AI action planner, and car controls commands issuance.

Let's not have an AI self-driving car that suddenly opts to swerve the car unexpectedly or slam on the brakes, doing so in the manner that a human might uncontrollably button or unbutton a sweater, all of which arises due to an alien limb syndrome.

Properly developed AI systems for self-driving cars need to be prepared for detecting and acting upon an alien limb and do so quickly and prior to allowing an alien limb to cause an untoward action.

That's good "medical advice" for those auto makers and tech firms that are developing AI self-driving cars and need a nudge to make sure they are being watchful for a Dr. Strangelove that might arise in their vaunted self-driving cars.

CHAPTER 8
JAYWALKING
AND
AI SELF-DRIVING CARS

CHAPTER 8

JAYWALKING
AND
AI SELF-DRIVING CARS

I remember one of the first times that I visited New York City (NYC) and made the mistake of renting a car to get around the famous metropolis. I had figured that driving a car around the avenues and streets would give me a solid sense of how the city that never sleeps was laid out and where the most notable restaurants, bars, and shops could be found.

Turns out that I mainly discovered how much New Yorkers seemed to delight in jaywalking. It was as though there weren't any rules against jaywalking. Want to cut across the street and get over to that popular hangout, no need to walk down to a crosswalk, instead just make your way by walking into traffic. In most cases, the jaywalker didn't even run. One might almost think that you would dart rather than kind of meander, but these fearless jaywalkers tended to take their time.

I also found out about the starring techniques that appeared to be a local custom. In some cities, the jaywalker does not make eye contact with the car drivers, seemingly acting as though the car drivers don't exist. Or, maybe by making eye contact it would become a duel to see who looked away first, and the loser perhaps has to back-down from the standoff.

In any case, my experience was that the jaywalkers loved to give the car drivers a straight eye. This might be the same kind of thing you'd do when you encounter a wild animal in the woods. Given them a strong stare might say that you are mighty and the animal should not try to take you on. Some of the car drivers that were locals or that were used to the local customs would often give a stern stare back. On a few occasions, it would get really testy and the jaywalker would wave an arm and act as though they might try to slay the dragon of a car coming down the street.

I admit that after I turned in the rental car and became more of a traditional pedestrian on my visits to NYC, I adopted the jaywalking habit. This was especially so because during one of my initial forays as a pedestrian there, I was walking with a colleague that was a native New Yorker, and when I attempted to walk down to a crosswalk, rather than taking the shortcut of jaywalking, he almost came out of his skin at my legal abiding approach. Are you nuts, he asked or demanded incredulously? Walk half a block down, cross the street at a light, and walk a half block back up, just to get to something that you could make a beeline to? I regret that perhaps it gave another black eye in his NYC mindset of my being from California.

He even justified the jaywalking in a manner that perhaps most would not. He insisted that it was actually more dangerous to cross at a marked crosswalk, at least in NYC, than it was to jaywalk. I doubt that he had any actual statistics to back the claim, but it certainly sounded convincing. He had me watch the cars turning at a busy corner and pointed out that I would seemingly be more likely to get run over there. With a jaywalking maneuver, he emphasized that I could pick my own choosing of when and where to cross, presumably therefore somehow being a much safer adventure than depending upon an actual marked crosswalk.

Where I grew up in California, jaywalking was generally frowned upon and only undertaken as some kind of last resort. If you had a bum leg and could not walk all the way to a corner, okay, maybe you could do a jaywalk, but only if the street was absolutely clear of traffic. No frogger kind of playing in my neighborhood. I remember my parents even hinting that the cops would likely be driving down the street just as I might try to jaywalk. This made me envision a life of sitting in prison due to having gotten caught red-handed doing a jaywalk. I wondered whether I would do hard time and also if I might ever be able to make parole due to the seriousness of my transgression against societies rules.

One time, a relative from New York came out to visit and noticed that some of the streets in my neighborhood had a posted sign that indicated jaywalking was prohibited. First, he laughed at the sign and declared it to be a total waste of taxpayer money. Second, he interpreted the sign to imply that wherever there wasn't a similar sign, it meant that you could legally jaywalk, and do so as much as your heart might desire. I tried to explain that jaywalking was generally outlawed locally and the purpose for the signs was to highlight the law, particularly in places where it was known that people tended to jaywalk, even though they weren't supposed to do so, and serve as a reminder of the law.

Since I had not seen much jaywalking growing up, it was fascinating to watch it occur while I had various stays in NYC. I noticed for example that the time of day seemed to make a difference in terms of the volume and nature of the jaywalking. Mornings, when pedestrians were trying to get to work, often stoked a lot of jaywalking, perhaps to try and get to work promptly and minimize the time required to get to the office.

There was also the amount of traffic that played a role in the jaywalking. If the traffic on a given street was completely backed-up and unmoving, jaywalkers would in droves weave in and around the cars, doing so without a care in the world since they perceived that the wild animals (the cars and car drivers) were jammed in place and couldn't do much to run them over. As soon as a green light allowed the traffic to flow, the jaywalkers became more cautious and realized it was now "game on" in terms of trying to time when to best engage in jaywalking.

If a street had intermittent traffic, and if the cars that used the street considered it be a kind of race track to quickly make some progress through the slew of blocks of NYC, the jaywalker had to be much more nimble and aware. Will that car that just turned onto the street be burning rubber and get to where you are going to jaywalk, reaching an intersecting point of the middle of the street just as you are halfway done with your jaywalk maneuver? These crazed drivers made it appear that they were not going to stop for anything and nor anyone. I don't care if you had your pet elephant on a leash and were jaywalking with it, these mean looking and solemn minded drivers were willing to smash their car into whatever might be in the roadway. The road was there's and no one dare suggest otherwise.

The weather also played a part in the jaywalking ritual. Rainy days meant that the jaywalkers had an even greater incentive to jaywalk. Why waste time and get wet in the rain, when you can scoot across a street and do so quickly enough that perhaps rain drops themselves won't touch you. The problem with the feverish effort to jaywalk in rain was the car drivers were likely to also be more crazed than usual. I suppose this was because the rain tended to hamper traffic and therefore the way to make-up for it was to speed and be a bit more careless of your driving. I realize you might assume it should be the opposite, namely you would slow down in the rain and be more careful, but that's not often the choice that drivers seem to make (this almost seems like a universal constant!).

At times, I pondered the nuances of Mutually Assured Destruction (MAD), which you might remember was popularized during the Cold War era. When the two hunkering superpowers of the United States and the Soviet Union had their nuclear arms race, it was postulated that if either one attacked, the other would surely attack, and in the end they would both obliterate each other.

This came to mind as I watched some of the jaywalking duels in NYC. An energetic jaywalker would enter into the street. A zealous driver would gun their engine and seem to aim for the jaywalker. Which would win the race?

I'm sure you are pleading that obviously the car will win, since a mere human is not going to have super powers to stop the car in its track. In that sense, certainly the car can always prevail by running over the human. You might think that's what would happen. Instead, it was interesting that even the nuttiest of drivers seemed to realize that running over a jaywalker was not an advisable thing to do.

Presumably, the car driver might be thinking that they could possibly get prosecuted for running over a jaywalker. Or, maybe they were worried it would dent their beloved car. Or, they might be concerned that their insurance rates would get jacked sky high. There's also the possibility that the driver might not want to maim a fellow human being. Well, being realistic, I'm putting that on the bottom of the list of reasons why the drivers did not summarily run over the jaywalkers.

So, it was often a Mutually Assured Destruction kind of battle. The jaywalker figured that the driver figured that hitting the jaywalker would not be a good thing to do. The driver figured that the jaywalker figured that getting hit by a car was not a good thing to have happen. Either way, if a physical connection was going to be made, it was a lousy outcome for both parties.

Some of the jaywalkers acted as though they had a special invisible shield that would protect them. They would walk across the street whenever they darned wished to do so. They seemed to believe that the drivers would ultimately acquiesce and not want to run over a jaywalker. Admittedly, this did seem to work a lot of the time.

When I mentioned to one of my NYC colleagues that the Mutually Assured Destruction won't serve as a deterrent unless both parties are cognizant and aware of what is taking place, he shrugged it off. I was trying to explain that if say the driver is not paying attention to the road, and not especially cognizant of the presence of the jaywalker, the driver could ram into the jaywalker out of "ignorance" and the jaywalker's expectation of being protected by MAD went out the window. The MAD approach only worked if the driver was truly paying attention to the road.

In my estimation, there seemed to be a sizable chunk of drivers that were not atune to the presence of the jaywalkers. This made sense since the drivers were having to contend with bigger game, such as large trucks trying to make deliveries and rapidly exiting and entering unexpectedly into the street and avenues. There were other crazed car drivers jockeying for position. There were often obstacles on the roadway such as a pallet of liquor bottles being delivered to a liquor store.

If you were a driver in that environment, which is a more suitable aspect to pay attention to? The trucks and other cars are likely more harmful to you and your car. The solid obstacles on pallets could do some real damage to your car if you hit them. A jaywalker? Not the highest priority.

Furthermore, many of the drivers seemed to consider that a jaywalker did jaywalking at their own risk. In essence, the car driver did not have to pay attention to the jaywalkers because the jaywalkers were "required" to always make sure to avoid getting hit by a car. It was as though a flock of birds were flying around the cars. A driver shouldn't have to watch out for the birds. The birds should be astute enough to not flap into a car. The jaywalkers were assumed to be hopefully as astute as a dumb bird.

Another factor involved sizing up the jaywalker. How was the jaywalker dressed and what kind of a look did they have? If a driver saw a jaywalker that seemed like a seasoned New Yorker, it suggested that the jaywalker could take care of themselves and no further driver attention was needed. If the jaywalker looked like a wide-eyed tourist, well, this might present a problem because the "amateur" jaywalker might foul things up. The "professional" jaywalkers knew how to assiduously cross a street. Those out-of-towner jaywalkers were bound to mess-up the delicate dance of true jaywalkers and NYC drivers.

I'm sure that when I drove my rental car, the jaywalkers could sense my out-of-town smell. Fresh meat, easy pickin's. I was the type that they could jaywalk to their hearts content on. Indeed, when I saw a jaywalker, I tended to give them a wide berth. The seasoned NYC drivers in contrast would always relish getting within inches of the jaywalker, as though it was a sweet kiss of "you just made it" and the jaywalker should thank their lucky stars for surviving the jaywalking act (and bend down in reverence to the car driver).

When it got somewhat late at night, I observed that there would be a segment of jaywalkers that were a bit intoxicated, having visited their preferred pub for some after-work libation. This seemed to dampen their wits as jaywalkers. I'm betting that they would contest this claim and say that they were still on their toes. In any case, there were definitely more close-calls on the jaywalker versus car aspects. This might also be further fueled by the likelihood of having drivers that were now also somewhat drunk. A potent combination, having both slightly drunk jaywalkers and slightly drunk drivers.

In most cases, I observed individuals acting as jaywalkers. This though was not always the case and there were frequently situations of multiple jaywalkers proceeding all at once. There was at times a herd mentality. If one of the jaywalkers went for it, the others were sure to follow. Now, this actually often made sense, since the first one likely found an opening to jaywalk and the others also perceived the same opening.

There were times though that the first jaywalker got the herd underway, not necessarily overtly, more so subliminally in that the other jaywalkers saw the first one make a move and opted to proceed too, but it turned out that the first jaywalker didn't gauge things well. The first jaywalker might have gotten somewhat stranded in the street, not able to fully make it across the street just yet. Meanwhile, the herd that followed was also now stranded. You could see the look on their faces that they had assumed they could make it fully across the street and were befuddled and irked that the move had not been timed well.

There were some of the "leaders" of the pack that weren't thinking at all about the rest of the herd. Therefore, they were not trying to find a big enough opening to get a dozen people across the street all at once. They were focusing on just themselves. In that case, sometimes the first mover made it across, but the others did not, and they had somehow assumed that if the first mover could do it, the rest of them could.

I suppose you could see this as a series of locking mechanisms that just happen to line-up precisely in a moment of time. The first mover has "calculated" that they can thin there way through the sporadic cars and make it across. It is though just a moment in time action. A split second later and the opportunity has vanished. Likewise, the alignment of the cars is not just a moment in time, but also a moment in space, as it were. The first mover at their position say halfway of the block, would have a different timing and clearance of an opening, versus if you were at a quarter way of the block.

The ones that got my heart pumping were situations in which two people were holding hands and opted to rush across the street together. As you can imagine, trying to get two people across on a precisely timed jaywalk is a lot more complex. If one of the two falters it can defeat the open window and you now have to figure out what to do. It was surprising at times to see how much connectedness was retained by the two.

In other words, two people are holding hands. This is obviously just a temporary connection in that their two hands are not glued to each other. They can separate their hands whenever they wish. And yet, in some cases, the pair would try to remain entangled, in spite of the danger of doing so. Just a mere dropping of their hands would allow them both to become free agents and more nimbly finish the jaywalk.

This though seemed to be the further most thought in some of their minds. It was as though the separating of their hands meant more to them than the chances of getting hit by a car. Was it true love that kept them together in that life risk move? Was it concern that the other one might feel abandoned and it could forever undermine their relationship? Maybe it was out of deep caring and the belief that by sticking together they could survive anything, including a crazed driver barreling down the street directly at them.

There's another kind of coupling sometimes that occurs, involving a jaywalker that is jaywalking with their dog. The jaywalking human might be hand carrying the dog, having lifted the dog up and embracing the animal like you would carry a football. This makes sense in that having the dog walk on a leash is going to be much more uncontrollable as you make your way across the street. For those that don't try to carry their dog, perhaps due to the weight and size of the dog, the leash approach can be quite dicey.

I remember seeing a man walking his dog that had a leash several feet long and as the man attempted to jaywalk, the dog tried to go in a different direction. This meant that the jaywalker was now several feet wide, if you consider the distance from him to his dog, making it much harder to nimbly get across the street. He pulled strenuously on the leash, nearly dragging the dog, as he desperately tried to bridge the chasm from one side of the street to the other.

In this case, he was somewhat strongly coupled because letting go of the leash would have produced perhaps even worse results. The dog might have scampered directly into traffic that otherwise the jaywalking human might have aided the dog in avoiding. All in all, I would say that any animal lovers would look upon these jaywalkers with some disdain, as it is one thing to put your own life into jeopardy and quite another to subject an innocent dog to the same kind of risk.

This reminds me too of a common refrain that my New York colleagues would use on me. They would say that any jaywalker is making their own decisions and if they get hit, well, that's their own doing. Why should the government tell them what they can and cannot do. It's up to the individual to choose to jaywalk or not, and it is on the head of that jaywalker as to whether they risk their life and limb or not.

I don't buy into this claim per se. It seems to leave the car drivers out of the equation. If a car driver hits a jaywalker, it's going to be a great deal of difficulty for the car driver, though yes I agree it is unlikely the car driver will be killed, but they could get injured. Furthermore, suppose the car driver is so anxious to avoid hitting a wayward jaywalker that the driver rams into another car? Now, you've got other people also enmeshed into the jaywalking effort.

There is also a chance that while the car driver is trying to avoid a jaywalker, the driver swerves and maybe hits other jaywalkers (I realize the view would be that's on them, if you take the individualist free agent perspective), or might come onto the curb and hit pedestrians (one would argue those pedestrians were innocents).

Generally, a jaywalker can start a cascading series of events that ultimately lead to others getting injured or killed. I therefore tend to reject the idea that a jaywalker is performing a "victimless" act, assuming that you don't count the jaywalker as a victim, and contend that the jaywalker is potentially going to involve one or more car drivers, perhaps one or more passengers in those involved cars, maybe other jaywalkers, and potentially innocent pedestrians that were mindfully using the sidewalk.

Here's another angle for you. What about the children?

I've seen jaywalkers holding the hand of a child or a group of children and trying to make a jaywalking attempt with them. Similar to my earlier point about coupling between two adults, in theory the coupling is loose since the hands can be disengaged readily. In the case of children, the danger obviously is that if the adult jaywalker does let go of the hands of the children involved, the children might not know what to do and get themselves into worse hot water.

I realize some would argue that of course the adult needs to hold the hands of the children and would accuse me of somehow suggesting that children should roam freely as jaywalkers. Let's be serious, I'm not implying that children should be unescorted by an adult when jaywalking. The thing is that children should not be jaywalking at all.

I'll probably get emails from some readers that will say that their children have "no choice" but to jaywalk and so which will it be, the children do so on their own or with an adult? I guess if there is really no other viable way to get to someplace other than jaywalking, yes, an adult jaywalker participant is the way to go. Is it really the case that there is no other viable way to get to the location other than jaywalking?

There are some that have said to me that it would require walking several added blocks and take another 15 minutes to get to the desired location, such as a school. Well, one has to then consider the ROI (Return on Investment) of walking those extra blocks and using those added 15 minutes, doing so presumably in a safer manner, versus the risks associated of doing the beeline jaywalking. Is there an appropriate risk/reward that says the added risk to the child makes the jaywalking act worthwhile?

One other qualm about involving children into jaywalking is the aspect that they essentially then come to believe that jaywalking is acceptable. If they do jaywalking with an adult, it is a slippery slope that can readily assume they can do jaywalking on their own. Indeed, some children will happily do jaywalking to showcase to their parent that they are now sentient and their own agent and no longer need to have an adult aid them in the jaywalking. It is a kind of rites of passage.

The counter argument from some adults is that if they don't show the child how to "properly" jaywalk, the odds are that the child is going to do jaywalking anyway at some point, and without having done so with a "responsible" adult, the child is going to be more prone to getting hurt when trying to do jaywalking based on no prior instruction. Some would say that having a head-in-the-sand viewpoint of being a parent that pretends jaywalking will never happen, will merely make the child more vulnerable than if you instead do a parent-child jaywalking effort with the child.

There are some aspects of the counter-argument that I do tend to side with. In the case of my own children, I did practice doing jaywalking with them, which I did to point out how to do so and what to watch out for. This was done though on a selective basis and only as a means to aid them in being prepared in case jaywalking was needed at some point. I tried to make clear cut that jaywalking was considered inappropriate and that the instruction was not meant to open the sport of jaywalking to them.

This also gets to the core of an aspect about children and child rearing. For those of you with children, you've likely been torn about whether to show or explain something to the child, for which you wonder whether you are introducing them to something that will spur them to do the thing you are trying to showcase should not be done. The classic is "don't put your hand in a stovetop burner," which could backfire in that the child might not have thought to do so, and now they are curious to try it, because you made such a big deal about it.

In any case, another facet of jaywalking is the possibility of adult jaywalkers, child jaywalkers, and combinations of both adult and child aged jaywalkers.

There's the special twist of the jaywalker that drops something while in the act of jaywalking. I saw a jaywalker that was carrying his coat as he darted across the street. The street was slightly wet from leftover rain. The person slipped while running across the street. As he regained his balance, he dropped his coat. At this point, his presumed prior calculated time to get across the street had been used up. A car was fast approaching. Should he pick-up his coat, which would take a precious second or two, and tempt fate with the ongoing car, or should he abandon the coat and safely get to the sidewalk.

Which is better, a coat that perhaps gets trampled by a moving car, and for which you can go out the street once the car has passed, readily pick-up the coat, and maybe get it dry cleaned to fix it up, or do you bend over while in the middle of the street and watch the ongoing car like it is a bull charging at you in Pamplona?

The answer seemed to be that nearly every time this kind of dropping action happened, the person opted to try and pick-up the dropped item. Was this out of a sense of personal affiliation with the dropped item? Maybe the coat had been in the family for many generations and was revered heirloom. Or due to the value? Perhaps it was an expensive coat from a top-end retailer. Or, could it be that the jaywalker was worried that the car driver might swerve to avoid the dropped item and therefore get into a wreck by having left it in the street? I doubt this is the first thought that goes through the mind of the jaywalker that dropped an item.

A car driver that witnesses a jaywalker dropping an item will need to figure out whether the jaywalker is going to try and stay in the street to retrieve it, or leave it there for later retrieval, or perhaps do some other kind of action now that the dropped item is there. The driver also needs to anticipate that maybe some other potential jaywalker might enter into the street to rescue the item for the first jaywalker that dropped the item. Whatever item has been dropped, the driver also needs to decide whether to try and brake before hitting it, if there is a chance of hitting it, or maybe try to straddle the item, or take some other kind of evasive driving action.

I've been so far primarily describing the jaywalkers and you'll notice that I've now started to shift focus toward the car drivers and the act of jaywalking pedestrians.

In terms of the drivers, there are drivers that know the jaywalking game and play it to the finest detail. There are the drivers that are driving while distracted and so inadvertently can be more menacing for a jaywalker. There are the drivers that are drunk or otherwise somewhat incapacitated and therefore are impaired while playing the jaywalking game. There are also the vendetta drivers.

I cannot say for sure that vendetta drivers really have a vendetta, though it certainly seems like it. Allow me to explain. I would see a potential "vendetta" driver driving down a street at a relatively constant pace. I am pretty sure they intended to remain at that pace. A jaywalker suddenly comes into the street. The jaywalker has calculated that they can make it across before the car comes upon them. Suddenly, the car speeds up.

Was the driver speeding up by chance alone? Did the driver just remember that they were late to a baseball game and opted to hit the gas? Or, was it that the driver saw the jaywalker and purposely wanted to give the jaywalker a scare? Suppose you are a driver that has reached your personal threshold with those darned jaywalkers. You might decide that whenever you see one, you will show them who is the boss. You speed up and see how close you can cut it to nearly hitting the jaywalker. In fact, if the jaywalker backs away, you are perhaps just as happy and feel like you did your civic duty.

Here's something else that seems to go into the jaywalking equation. Does the jaywalker have any kind of encumbrance like a heavy backpack, or maybe a briefcase, or carrying a box or some other object? This tends to slow down the jaywalker and requires them to find a somewhat wider opening in terms of time and space. You might think of this as a kind of golf-like handicap.

Some jaywalkers did not appear to include their encumbrance in their jaywalking formulation. Whereas before they could more readily make a window of X and Y, they know could only do a Q and Z, but they seemed to still be making a jaywalking move when it was only an X and Y window. Danger ensued. Likewise, the drivers would sometimes misjudge the pace and agility of the jaywalker, getting darned close, closer than it seemed they intended, partially because they also miscalculated the delay factor of the encumbrance of the jaywalker.

Nighttime jaywalking was somewhat akin to daylight jaywalking as long as the street was well lit (assuming everyone involved was sober). On some NYC streets, the lighting is not so good. This increased the chances of sour encounters between jaywalkers and drivers. The jaywalker at times seemed to think that the darkness was handy, hiding their jaywalking transgression. The drivers were less likely to see the jaywalkers and get started when the headlights of the car shone upon an unexpected jaywalker.

You can combine together all of my aforementioned factors and make the jaywalking into a rather complicated game of human versus human. Human jaywalkers that have human frailties and can misjudge when and how to jaywalk. Weather conditions that can impact the game, along with daylight versus darkness. Drivers that pay attention and other drivers that do not. Some that have a vendetta, some that are drunk.

It's a real mishmash. Overall, it is kind of startling and amazing that there aren't more injuries and deaths due to jaywalking, especially in cities that take jaywalking for granted and it doesn't get suppressed or expunged.

Of course, not all countries are necessarily opposed to jaywalking. On an international basis, there are some places in the world that jaywalking is strictly forbidden, and other places that allow it and give no special heed about it. You might find of idle interest that the root word "jay" essentially means inexperienced, and when cars first came onto roadways there were drivers that drove on the wrong side of the street, which were referred to as jay-drivers. This morphed eventually into becoming jaywalkers.

Who has the proper right of way?

In some countries, both the jaywalker and the driver are considered equals in terms of right-of-way. Once a jaywalker starts across the street, in some countries this implies that the jaywalker now has the true right-of-way, subject to whether the jaywalker has made a sensible move or not. If the jaywalker steps into the street in front of a car going 60 miles per hour and there was no chance for the driver to stop, the jaywalker cannot expect to have claimed right-of-way.

Here's what the Department of Motor Vehicles (DMV) rulebook in California states about the act of jaywalking:

"(a) Every pedestrian upon a roadway at any point other than within a marked crosswalk or within an unmarked crosswalk at an intersection shall yield the right-of-way to all vehicles upon the roadway so near as to constitute an immediate hazard.

(b) The provisions of this section shall not relieve the driver of a vehicle from the duty to exercise due care for the safety of any pedestrian upon a roadway."

You'll notice that the jaywalker is supposed to yield the right-of-way to cars. Notice further that in spite of that aspect, it does mean that a driver can just run over a jaywalker. The driver must also exercise due care, even if a jaywalker is doing something they aren't supposed to be doing.

What does this have to do with AI self-driving cars?

At the Cybernetic AI Self-Driving Car Institute, we are developing AI software for self-driving cars. One crucial aspect involves the AI being able to contend with jaywalkers.

Allow me to elaborate.

I'd like to clarify and introduce the notion that there are varying levels of AI self-driving cars. The topmost level is considered Level 5. A Level 5 self-driving car is one that is being driven by the AI and there is no human driver involved. For the design of Level 5 self-driving cars, the auto makers are even removing the gas pedal, brake pedal, and steering wheel, since those are contraptions used by human drivers. The Level 5 self-driving car is not being driven by a human and nor is there an expectation that a human driver will be present in the self-driving car. It's all on the shoulders of the AI to drive the car.

For self-driving cars less than a Level 5, there must be a human driver present in the car. The human driver is currently considered the responsible party for the acts of the car. The AI and the human driver are co-sharing the driving task. In spite of this co-sharing, the human is supposed to remain fully immersed into the driving task and be ready at all times to perform the driving task. I've repeatedly warned about the dangers of this co-sharing arrangement and predicted it will produce many untoward results.

Let's focus herein on the true Level 5 self-driving car. Much of the comments apply to the less than Level 5 self-driving cars too, but the fully autonomous AI self-driving car will receive the most attention in this discussion.

Here's the usual steps involved in the AI driving task:
- Sensor data collection and interpretation
- Sensor fusion
- Virtual world model updating
- AI action planning
- Car controls command issuance

Another key aspect of AI self-driving cars is that they will be driving on our roadways in the midst of human driven cars too. There are some pundits of AI self-driving cars that continually refer to a utopian world in which there are only AI self-driving cars on the public roads. Currently there are about 250+ million conventional cars in the United States alone, and those cars are not going to magically disappear or become true Level 5 AI self-driving cars overnight.

Indeed, the use of human driven cars will last for many years, likely many decades, and the advent of AI self-driving cars will occur while there are still human driven cars on the roads. This is a crucial point since this means that the AI of self-driving cars needs to be able to contend with not just other AI self-driving cars, but also contend with human driven cars. It is easy to envision a simplistic and rather unrealistic world in which all AI self-driving cars are politely interacting with each other and being civil about roadway interactions. That's not what is going to be happening for the foreseeable future. AI self-driving cars and human driven cars will need to be able to cope with each other.

Returning to the topic of jaywalkers, let's consider the capabilities that an AI self-driving car should have regarding contending with these wayward pedestrians.

I'll tackle right away a comment that I sometimes get from AI developers. There are some that say there is no need for an AI self-driving car to do anything at all about a jaywalker. Jaywalkers are acting illegally. They get whatever they deserve. There is no requirement that the AI of the self-driving car needs to do anything at all about a jaywalker.

It might seem astonishing to you that someone would think this way. It is a phenomenon that I refer to as the "egocentric" developer viewpoint. The world needs to conform to their view of the world, rather than the developer facing the reality of the real-world. I quickly point out to such a person that the DMV code clearly states that the car driver must exercise a duty of care, even if the jaywalker is doing something utterly wrong and illegal.

This often surprises the AI developer. They had laid all of the responsibility onto the shoulders of the wayward pedestrian. In one sense, this is similar to the jaywalkers that insist they are doing a "victimless" act and that it is up to the jaywalker to choose whether to personally risk doing jaywalking or not. Only after I point out the other "victims" that can get dragged into the "victimless" effort do they (hopefully) see the larger picture.

Let's all assume that indeed the AI of the self-driving car does need to contend with jaywalkers. It cannot ignore them. It cannot pretend that the burden of safety is solely on the backs of the jaywalkers. The AI must have provisions for dealing with jaywalkers. I'd say that's a prudent and societally expected assumption about AI self-driving cars.

This moves us then into the next kind of quirk that some AI developers offer. There are some AI developers that will concede the notion of doing something about jaywalkers, but then argue that a jaywalker is nothing special and that the "normal" driving aspects of an AI self-driving car should suffice when dealing with jaywalkers.

In this case, the AI developer is suggesting that if the AI self-driving car is already prepared to cope with objects that might appear in the roadway, the job of having the AI be prepared for jaywalkers is already completed. No need to do anything else.

This implies that a jaywalker is no different from say a tumbleweed. If the AI is able to detect a tumbleweed in the roadway, it amounts to the same thing as detecting a human in the roadway. At least that's the kind of thinking involved by this kind of AI developer.

If I was driving my car and saw a tumbleweed in the road, I would likely mentally calculate whether to hit it or not. I might be willing to hit the tumbleweed due to the aspect that perhaps there are other cars near me and if I hit my brakes suddenly, I risk getting rear-ended, and maybe I cannot switch lanes without endangering a car adjacent to me, and maybe radically swerving is likewise going to endanger me and other nearby cars and pedestrians. So, I might choose to ram the tumbleweed, doing so as the "safest" option available to me at the time and moment that the tumbleweed has appeared.

Here's an easy question for you, I think, namely do you consider it viable to ram a jaywalker, using the same logic about ramming a tumbleweed? I'd dare say that you would be willing to take much greater chances to avoid hitting the jaywalker than you would hitting a tumbleweed. As an aside, this raises further the ethical aspects involved in driving a car. Suppose you can avoid the jaywalker but might end-up on the sidewalk and hit a pedestrian standing there – what is the basis for making such a choice, and how do we end-up embodying this kind of decision making into an AI system of a self-driving car?

Back to the object in the roadway problem, do we want AI self-driving cars that seem to equate hitting a human jaywalker is akin to hitting a tumbleweed? I don't believe we do.

Thus, I claim that if an AI system is only detecting "objects" and not trying to also figure out what kind of object is involved, it is insufficient in terms of what we would all hope a true AI self-driving car is going to be able to do. From a systems perspective, please realize that I realize that when the cameras, radar, LIDAR, and other sensors first do their detection, they are only indeed detecting "objects" and thus there is a crucial role of object detection involved. What I am saying is that after the raw sensory detection of an object, it is imperative that the AI system tries to discern what kind of object the object is, such as whether it is a tumbleweed or a human.

That's why the interplay of the sensory detection and sensor fusion is vital. When the AI system is trying to piece together the sensor data from multiple sensors, it has an enhanced chance of trying to ferret out what kind of object is being dealt with. This also interplays with the virtual world model. The virtual world model should be tracking the object over time, which will also then aid in trying to ascertain what the object might be. The AI action planning capability needs to be "astute" enough to be able to detect patterns of shapes and movement that pertain to humans and try to differentiate this from other kinds of objects.

I purposely have chosen the tumbleweed example because it is a tricky one to discern from the movements of a human. For example, you might say that a human should presumably start off the street and proceed into the street. Certainly, a tumbleweed could do the same. A jaywalker once in the street is going to likely be making their way across the street. A tumbleweed might do the same, perhaps the wind is pushing it in that direction.

A jaywalker might make a direct beeline across the street. A tumbleweed could do the same. A jaywalker might weave as they cross the street, and of course a tumbleweed might do the same. By the movement alone, you cannot necessarily say whether the object is a human trying to jaywalk versus a tumbleweed.

You would need to combine together a multitude of factors. What is the size and shape of the object? Does it resemble the size and shape of a human? Does it move in a seemingly directed fashion, but if so, can this be differentiated from the possible random movements of an object like a tumbleweed? We also need to consider whether the object might be an animal, which could move across the street in the same overall manner that a jaywalker might or a tumbleweed might.

Guessing whether or not the object is a jaywalker then opens an entire plethora of other aspects for the AI to consider. My stories about jaywalkers provides ample indication of the kinds of acts that a jaywalker might do. A car driver that is watching the road would indeed adjust their driving behavior based on the realization that a jaywalker is in the road. You might slow down, you might speed-up, you might honk your horn, you might do all kinds of actions as a driver. Likewise, the AI of a true AI self-driving car should be doing similar kinds of actions.

Auto makers and tech firms that are making AI self-driving cars are often dealing with just getting an AI self-driving car to deal with the rudiments of driving, and they would say that the best bet is to have the AI always assume the worst-case scenario. This means that a tumbleweed that might be a human is going to be assumed to be a human, which is considered a safer bet than not making that kind of assumption.

They would also tend toward having the AI take the "super-cautious" approach. I remember being invited to watch an AI self-driving car as it drove down an empty street, and the auto maker and tech firm had a stuntman walk out into the street, acting like a jaywalker. The AI was able to detect the jaywalker and came to a nearly immediate halt. Success!

Well, not exactly. The AI self-driving car came to a halt at about one quarter into the block, and the jaywalker was at the other quarter's end of the block. Sure, the AI self-driving car detected the jaywalker at a sizable distance and came to a prompt halt at a sizable distance. It was maybe just somewhat less than a half a football field away from the human when it halted. Great, no chance of hitting that person.

Does this make sense in the real-world? Imagine if AI self-driving cars are all coming to a grinding halt when detecting a human in the street when the human is many many car lengths away. Will this be a viable way for AI self-driving cars to make their way on our streets? Suppose all human drivers did the same. You might argue that we'd be safer, but I wonder about how this would really play out.

For example, if you knew that a human driver would always stop for you, wouldn't you nearly always choose to jaywalk? The moment you see a car coming down the street, just step into the street, and voila that car is going to come to a halt. You and others could pretty much paralyze all car traffic. Maybe we would end-up with far less jaywalking injuries and deaths, but what would it also do to our ability to use cars as a means of transportation?

There are already reports of people opting to "prank" today's AI self-driving cars. If you know that an AI self-driving car will stop or maybe turn when you take some kind of action as a pedestrian or maybe when driving in your own car, it is human nature that we would all likely exploit these behaviors of the AI self-driving cars. Want to get ahead and not be behind one of those slower moving AI self-driving cars, easy enough to arrange by tricking the AI self-driving car into slowing down or halting.

A true AI self-driving car has to be embodied with the kinds of driving skills that humans use, and particularly so with regard to contending with jaywalkers. It is insufficient to simply rely upon some kind of overarching object detection and assume that doing so will resolve how to cope with jaywalkers. That's not what human drivers seem to do. The behavior of human drivers is actually quite more complex, and we need to aim for having AI systems that can perform in a like manner.

The AI system needs to incorporate the multitude of factors that I've previously mentioned. Is the suspected jaywalker an adult or a child? Is it one person or more than one person? Is there a coupling between the multiple jaywalkers? Might the jaywalker drop something into the roadway, and if so, what contingencies should be considered? Does the weather increase or decrease the chances of jaywalking and is the street that you are driving on more or less prone to jaywalkers? And so on.

Some are hoping that the use of Machine Learning (ML) and Deep Learning (DL) will come to the aid of trying to cope with jaywalkers. In one sense, yes, it can be helpful to use ML and DL, and by collecting large sets of jaywalking circumstances begin to find patterns to suggest how jaywalkers behave, and therefore then have ready-made solutions in-hand by the AI.

I assure you though that today's kind of ML and DL is not going to be the silver bullet or magic wand that provides the jaywalking kind of driving aptitude needed for a true AI self-driving car. The jaywalker aspects are far too complex. It is not the same as merely analyzing an image to ferret out whether there is a human in the scene or not. This has to do with behaviors and complex ones.

Conclusion

Most seasoned drivers tend to take jaywalkers in stride (pun!), meaning that we human drivers can detect jaywalkers, we can anticipate what they might do, we can adjust our driving aspects accordingly, and most of the time the dance leads to the jaywalker getting safely across the street and the car safety proceeding down the street. This is nearly an effortless act by a seasoned human driver.

AI self-driving cars are not yet as prepared for handling jaywalkers. The sad incident of the jaywalker in Arizona being run down by an Uber self-driving car is but one example of how limited today's AI self-driving cars are in terms of coping with jaywalkers. We need to focus greater attention on the AI capability to specifically deal with jaywalkers and not allow the assumed everyday capabilities of the AI to be able to contend properly with jaywalking.

Why did the jaywalker cross the road? Answer: To safely get to the other side. Whether you live in a country or place that condones jaywalking or shuns it, in the real-world jaywalking exists and will continue to exist.

Here in Los Angeles, they have started a new effort to discourage jaywalking. If a jaywalker is caught jaywalking and it is their first such caught offence, Los Angeles will give them a bright colored vest and an LED light for free, and tell them that if they continue to jaywalk, which they are not supposed to do, they should at least wear the vest and hold the LED light up (and no ticket for jaywalking is issued). You might think this a rather "odd" kind of solution to the problem of jaywalking. Some think it is ingenious, others think it is outright ludicrous.

Let's be safe out there, and the AI needs to be part of that safety mindset.

.

APPENDIX

APPENDIX A
TEACHING WITH THIS MATERIAL

The material in this book can be readily used either as a supplemental to other content for a class, or it can also be used as a core set of textbook material for a specialized class. Classes where this material is most likely used include any classes at the college or university level that want to augment the class by offering thought provoking and educational essays about AI and self-driving cars.

In particular, here are some aspects for class use:

o   <u>Computer Science</u>. Studying AI, autonomous vehicles, etc.

o   <u>Business</u>. Exploring technology and it adoption for business.

o   <u>Sociology</u>. Sociological views on the adoption and advancement of technology.

Specialized classes at the undergraduate and graduate level can also make use of this material.

For each chapter, consider whether you think the chapter provides material relevant to your course topic. There is plenty of opportunity to get the students thinking about the topic and force them to decide whether they agree or disagree with the points offered and positions taken. I would also encourage you to have the students do additional research beyond the chapter material presented (I provide next some suggested assignments they can do).

RESEARCH ASSIGNMENTS ON THESE TOPICS

Your students can find background material on these topics, doing so in various business and technical publications. I list below the top ranked AI related journals. For business publications, I would suggest the usual culprits such as the Harvard Business Review, Forbes, Fortune, WSJ, and the like.

Here are some suggestions of homework or projects that you could assign to students:

a) Assignment for foundational AI research topic: Research and prepare a paper and a presentation on a specific aspect of Deep AI, Machine Learning, ANN, etc. The paper should cite at least 3 reputable sources. Compare and contrast to what has been stated in this book.

b) Assignment for the Self-Driving Car topic: Research and prepare a paper and Self-Driving Cars. Cite at least 3 reputable sources and analyze the characterizations. Compare and contrast to what has been stated in this book.

c) Assignment for a Business topic: Research and prepare a paper and a presentation on businesses and advanced technology. What is hot, and what is not? Cite at least 3 reputable sources. Compare and contrast to the depictions in this book.

d) Assignment to do a Startup: Have the students prepare a paper about how they might startup a business in this realm. They must submit a sound Business Plan for the startup. They could also be asked to present their Business Plan and so should also have a presentation deck to coincide with it.

You can certainly adjust the aforementioned assignments to fit to your particular needs and the class structure. You'll notice that I ask for 3 reputable cited sources for the paper writing based assignments. I usually steer students toward "reputable" publications, since otherwise they will cite some oddball source that has no credentials other than that they happened to write something and post it onto the Internet. You can define "reputable" in whatever way you prefer, for example some faculty think Wikipedia is not reputable while others believe it is reputable and allow students to cite it.

The reason that I usually ask for at least 3 citations is that if the student only does one or two citations they usually settle on whatever they happened to find the fastest. By requiring three citations, it usually seems to force them to look around, explore, and end-up probably finding five or more, and then whittling it down to 3 that they will actually use.

I have not specified the length of their papers, and leave that to you to tell the students what you prefer. For each of those assignments, you could end-up with a short one to two pager, or you could do a dissertation length paper. Base the length on whatever best fits for your class, and the credit amount of the assignment within the context of the other grading metrics you'll be using for the class.

I mention in the assignments that they are to do a paper and prepare a presentation. I usually try to get students to present their work. This is a good practice for what they will do in the business world. Most of the time, they will be required to prepare an analysis and present it. If you don't have the class time or inclination to have the students present, then you can of course cut out the aspect of them putting together a presentation.

If you want to point students toward highly ranked journals in AI, here's a list of the top journals as reported by *various citation counts sources* (this list changes year to year):

- Communications of the ACM
- Artificial Intelligence
- Cognitive Science
- IEEE Transactions on Pattern Analysis and Machine Intelligence
- Foundations and Trends in Machine Learning
- Journal of Memory and Language
- Cognitive Psychology
- Neural Networks
- IEEE Transactions on Neural Networks and Learning Systems
- IEEE Intelligent Systems
- Knowledge-based Systems

GUIDE TO USING THE CHAPTERS

For each of the chapters, I provide next some various ways to use the chapter material. You can assign the tasks as individual homework assignments, or the tasks can be used with team projects for the class. You can easily layout a series of assignments, such as indicating that the students are to do item "a" below for say Chapter 1, then "b" for the next chapter of the book, and so on.

a) What is the main point of the chapter and describe in your own words the significance of the topic,

b) Identify at least two aspects in the chapter that you agree with, and support your concurrence by providing at least one other outside researched item as support; make sure to explain your basis for disagreeing with the aspects,

c) Identify at least two aspects in the chapter that you disagree with, and support your disagreement by providing at least one other outside researched item as support; make sure to explain your basis for disagreeing with the aspects,

d) Find an aspect that was not covered in the chapter, doing so by conducting outside research, and then explain how that aspect ties into the chapter and what significance it brings to the topic,

e) Interview a specialist in industry about the topic of the chapter, collect from them their thoughts and opinions, and readdress the chapter by citing your source and how they compared and contrasted to the material,

f) Interview a relevant academic professor or researcher in a college or university about the topic of the chapter, collect from them their thoughts and opinions, and readdress the chapter by citing your source and how they compared and contrasted to the material,

g) Try to update a chapter by finding out the latest on the topic, and ascertain whether the issue or topic has now been solved or whether it is still being addressed, explain what you come up with.

The above are all ways in which you can get the students of your class involved in considering the material of a given chapter. You could mix things up by having one of those above assignments per each week, covering the chapters over the course of the semester or quarter.

As a reminder, here are the chapters of the book and you can select whichever chapters you find most valued for your particular class:

Companion Book By This Author

Advances in AI and Autonomous Vehicles: Cybernetic Self-Driving Cars

Practical Advances in Artificial Intelligence (AI) and Machine Learning

by

Dr. Lance B. Eliot, MBA, PhD

This title is available via Amazon and other book sellers

Companion Book By This Author

Self-Driving Cars:
"The Mother of All AI Projects"

by Dr. Lance B. Eliot, MBA, PhD

Chapter Title

This title is available via Amazon and other book sellers

Companion Book By This Author

Innovation and Thought Leadership
on Self-Driving Driverless Cars

by Dr. Lance B. Eliot, MBA, PhD

This title is available via Amazon and other book sellers

Companion Book By This Author

New Advances in AI Autonomous
Driverless Cars Self-Driving Cars

by Dr. Lance B. Eliot, MBA, PhD

Chapter Title

This title is available via Amazon and other book sellers

Companion Book By This Author
Introduction to
Driverless Self-Driving Cars
by Dr. Lance B. Eliot, MBA, PhD

This title is available via Amazon and other book sellers

Companion Book By This Author

Autonomous Vehicle Driverless Self-Driving Cars and Artificial Intelligence

by Dr. Lance B. Eliot, MBA, PhD

This title is available via Amazon and other book sellers

Companion Book By This Author

Transformative Artificial Intelligence Driverless Self-Driving Cars

by Dr. Lance B. Eliot, MBA, PhD

Chapter Title

This title is available via Amazon and other book sellers

Companion Book By This Author

Disruptive Artificial Intelligence and Driverless Self-Driving Cars

by Dr. Lance B. Eliot, MBA, PhD

Chapter Title

This title is available via Amazon and other book sellers

Companion Book By This Author

State-of-the-Art
AI Driverless Self-Driving Cars

by Dr. Lance B. Eliot, MBA, PhD

This title is available via Amazon and other book sellers

Companion Book By This Author

Top Trends in
AI Self-Driving Cars

by Dr. Lance B. Eliot, MBA, PhD

Chapter Title

This title is available via Amazon and other book sellers

Companion Book By This Author

AI Innovations
and Self-Driving Cars

by Dr. Lance B. Eliot, MBA, PhD

Chapter Title

This title is available via Amazon and other book sellers

Companion Book By This Author

Crucial Advances for
AI Self-Driving Cars

by Dr. Lance B. Eliot, MBA, PhD

This title is available via Amazon and other book sellers

Companion Book By This Author

Sociotechnical Insights and AI Driverless Cars

by Dr. Lance B. Eliot, MBA, PhD

<u>Chapter Title</u>

1 Eliot Framework for AI Self-Driving Cars

2 Start-ups and AI Self-Driving Cars

3 Code Obfuscation and AI Self-Driving Cars

4 Hyperlanes and AI Self-Driving Cars

5 Passenger Panic Inside an AI Self-Driving Car

6 Tech Stockholm Syndrome and Self-Driving Cars

7 Paralysis and AI Self-Driving Cars

8 Ugly Zones and AI Self-Driving Cars

9 Ridesharing and AI Self-Driving Cars

10 Multi-Party Privacy and AI Self-Driving Cars

11 Chaff Bugs and AI Self-Driving Cars

12 Social Reciprocity and AI Self-Driving Cars

13 Pet Mode and AI Self-Driving Cars

This title is available via Amazon and other book sellers

Companion Book By This Author

Pioneering Advances for AI Driverless Cars

by Dr. Lance B. Eliot, MBA, PhD

This title is available via Amazon and other book sellers

Companion Book By This Author

Leading Edge Trends for AI Driverless Cars

by Dr. Lance B. Eliot, MBA, PhD

This title is available via Amazon and other book sellers

Companion Book By This Author

The Cutting Edge of AI Autonomous Cars

by Dr. Lance B. Eliot, MBA, PhD

Chapter Title

This title is available via Amazon and other book sellers

Companion Book By This Author

The Next Wave of
AI Self-Driving Cars

by Dr. Lance B. Eliot, MBA, PhD

Chapter Title

1   Eliot Framework for AI Self-Driving Cars

2   Productivity and AI Self-Driving Cars

3   Blind Pedestrians and AI Self-Driving Cars

4   Fail-Safe AI and AI Self-Driving Cars

5   Anomaly Detection and AI Self-Driving Cars

6   Running Out of Gas and AI Self-Driving Cars

7   Deep Personalization and AI Self-Driving Cars

8   Reframing the Levels of AI Self-Driving Cars

9   Cryptojacking and AI Self-Driving Cars

This title is available via Amazon and other book sellers

Companion Book By This Author

Revolutionary Innovations of
AI Self-Driving Cars

by Dr. Lance B. Eliot, MBA, PhD

This title is available via Amazon and other book sellers

<u>Companion Book By This Author</u>

AI Self-Driving Cars
Breakthroughs

by Dr. Lance B. Eliot, MBA, PhD

<u>Chapter Title</u>

1 Eliot Framework for AI Self-Driving Cars

2 Off-Roading and AI Self-Driving Cars

3 Paralleling Vehicles and AI Self-Driving Cars

4 Dementia Drivers and AI Self-Driving Cars

5 Augmented Realty (AR) and AI Self-Driving Cars

6 Sleeping Inside an AI Self-Driving Car

7 Prevalence Detection and AI Self-Driving Cars

8 Super-Intelligent AI and AI Self-Driving Cars

9 Car Caravans and AI Self-Driving Cars

This title is available via Amazon and other book sellers

Companion Book By This Author

Trailblazing Trends for
AI Self-Driving Cars

by Dr. Lance B. Eliot, MBA, PhD

Chapter Title

This title is available via Amazon and other book sellers

Companion Book By This Author

Ingenious Strides for
AI Driverless Cars

by Dr. Lance B. Eliot, MBA, PhD

This title is available via Amazon and other book sellers

ABOUT THE AUTHOR

Dr. Lance B. Eliot, MBA, PhD is the CEO of Techbruim, Inc. and Executive Director of the Cybernetic AI Self-Driving Car Institute, and has over twenty years of industry experience including serving as a corporate officer in a billion dollar firm and was a partner in a major executive services firm. He is also a serial entrepreneur having founded, ran, and sold several high-tech related businesses. He previously hosted the popular radio show *Technotrends* that was also available on American Airlines flights via their in-flight audio program. Author or co-author of a dozen books and over 400 articles, he has made appearances on CNN, and has been a frequent speaker at industry conferences.

A former professor at the University of Southern California (USC), he founded and led an innovative research lab on Artificial Intelligence in Business. Known as the "AI Insider" his writings on AI advances and trends has been widely read and cited. He also previously served on the faculty of the University of California Los Angeles (UCLA), and was a visiting professor at other major universities. He was elected to the International Board of the Society for Information Management (SIM), a prestigious association of over 3,000 high-tech executives worldwide.

He has performed extensive community service, including serving as Senior Science Adviser to the Vice Chair of the Congressional Committee on Science & Technology. He has served on the Board of the OC Science & Engineering Fair (OCSEF), where he is also has been a Grand Sweepstakes judge, and likewise served as a judge for the Intel International SEF (ISEF). He served as the Vice Chair of the Association for Computing Machinery (ACM) Chapter, a prestigious association of computer scientists. Dr. Eliot has been a shark tank judge for the USC Mark Stevens Center for Innovation on start-up pitch competitions, and served as a mentor for several incubators and accelerators in Silicon Valley and Silicon Beach. He served on several Boards and Committees at USC, including having served on the Marshall Alumni Association (MAA) Board in Southern California.

Dr. Eliot holds a PhD from USC, MBA, and Bachelor's in Computer Science, and earned the CDP, CCP, CSP, CDE, and CISA certifications. Born and raised in Southern California, and having traveled and lived internationally, he enjoys scuba diving, surfing, and sailing.

ADDENDUM

Ingenious Strides for AI Driverless Cars

*Practical Advances in Artificial Intelligence (AI)
and Machine Learning*

By
Dr. Lance B. Eliot, MBA, PhD

———

For supplemental materials of this book, visit:
www.ai-selfdriving-cars.guru

For special orders of this book, contact:
LBE Press Publishing
Email: LBE.Press.Publishing@gmail.com

www.ingramcontent.com/pod-product-compliance
Lightning Source LLC
Chambersburg PA
CBHW051049050326
40690CB00006B/652